May 27, 2020

Dear Merrill,

    Thank you for your purchase.
We hope you find this worthwhile.
Much love,
Chuck and Nance

Acclaim for
KEVIN COURAGEOUS: A Journey of Faith, Hope and Love
By Mary Ann and Chuck Mansfield

Lucine Marous has commented, "The new book has much to say for itself. To begin, the Mansfield family has the benefit of awareness of the caring support of so many others for its well-being. It had to be challenging to renew all the dreadfully painful memories but it attests to the strength of familial love. The authors' daughter Katie seems to have inherited the family skill for words. Her poetry is quite touching.

"Although I had known of many of the messages and diagnoses before, there is a powerfulness in reading of all the support that others had offered, and continue to offer, which will someday, I'm sure, give great comfort to Kevin and his siblings. How beneficial it is to have such a reminder of the goodness of friends and strangers in the time of adversity. I believe this work also has the advantage of helping others who might be going through similar life challenges."

Award-winning novelist and essayist **Cynthia Ozick** has written, "I have by now fully absorbed the heart-piercing privilege of reading *KEVIN COURAGEOUS*. This beautiful, talented, witty, and joy-bringing young man! And how moving it is to see him embraced by the faithful devotion (in all senses) and wisdom and love of his parents and grandparents and sister Marissa and brothers Tim and Justin and aunt Kate (whose brave and fiery poem encompasses all)! No one who reads this heart-breaking yet ultimately glorious narrative of rising strength and risen trust will come away unchanged, knowing more fully than before the meaning of gratitude. The Mansfield family is proof that love (even when it is hard work in the face of peril) works. Thank you, thank you for allowing me entry into these fields of hurt and striving and coming through. And may Kevin, and Kevin's mother and father and all who cherish him, go from strength to strength."

Retired Registered Nurse **Kay Payne** has emailed, "I'm loving the Mansfields' new book! It's wonderful and inspiring, but also brings tears to my eyes! This book is a testament to the miraculous power of prayer and trusting in God to heal when faced with the grave, life-threatening illness of their beloved grandson. They have done a magnificent job of documenting the journey of Kevin's illness and his fight to recover from the damage. Emails from Dawn, Kevin's mother, who spent weeks at his bedside, gave a touching, daily account of the heart-wrenching struggle. Enlisting family and friends to cover Kevin in prayer and share in this journey has blessed even us 'prayer warriors.' The recovery Kevin has made is miraculous considering the severity of the necrotizing encephalitis. God truly does hear and answer our prayers!"

Heath Hardage Lee, author of *The League of Wives: The Untold Story of the Women Who Took on the U.S. Government to Bring Their Husbands Home from Vietnam*, has written, "Wow this was a tough read but a very uplifting one! The Mansfields' grandson is truly amazing and his recovery is miraculous. How hard this has been on all of them though. I am so sorry they all had to go through this. Nothing is worse than seeing a young person struck down by something so random and so devastating. What really came across here though is the love and support that Kevin is surrounded by. He is a lucky kid in that way!"

Retired CEO **James C. Norwood, Jr.** has emailed, "After reading your new work I was inspired to write this to all members of the Mansfield family: Joan and I can assure you that over the rest of the Mansfields' lives they will realize the blessing that God has given them with the tragic health burden He has wrought upon Kevin. We have experienced the birth of John Patrick, the fourth of our five children. John was born with Down Syndrome 44 years ago and his birth had similar impacts on our family as Kevin's health event has had and will continue to have. And today our family consists of 22 members including John's wife of 15 years, Alexis; and I defy anyone to find a more loving family unit on earth. Every one of us knows what it feels like to direct love, understanding and respect towards one of us who is disabled, and to feel the love back from him is the best feeling ever. So be ready, Mansfields. Hope, love and more. Love is on its way! Love forever!"

Thomas P. Kiley, Jr. has written: "In their latest literary exertion, *KEVIN COURAGEOUS*, the Mansfields have managed to tug at the heartstrings while revealing truths that are not often written about when writers put pen to paper, as in this case, to tell about a family coming together in troubled times to surround their stricken son/grandson with its strength, hope and, above all, its love. Smart lad their Kevin to give us through his suffering a gift that reaches out to all of us and teaches us things about life we once knew very well but have forgotten, and new things we would never have thought about if it were not for him. It is said that the triangle is the strongest geometric shape, but the Mansfields prove anew that a family's heart is even stronger. One thing is for certain. Once you start *KEVIN COURAGEOUS*, you'll be hard-pressed to put it down."

Dr. Dennis C. Golden, President Emeritus of Fontbonne University and a former Marine Corps officer, has written, "*KEVIN COURAGEOUS* (KC) is a book like none other because of the Mansfield family, the 'prayer warriors' et al. but most of all because of Kevin himself and his valiant battle as only the second person in the U.S. to have ANEM (ANE) as a direct result of the flu. This brought the members of 'Mansclan,' other family members, medical experts, friends, associates et al. to their knees in prayer. Then they stood straight and tall and committed themselves to overcoming one and all. As one KC reader, I found the book brought me through fears to tears and eventually cheers – for KEVIN as he raised the courage bar to the sky.

"The inclusion of the epic stories of Lt. "Sully" Sullivan and PFC John Devine gave me deeper insights into 'profiles in courage' and the 'true grit' to believe that 'We shall overcome.' Both Marissa's poem to her 'Little Brother' and the unconquerable theme in 'Invictus' brought brilliant strength and soul to KC.

"My initial misperceived anger and concern via the exchange of 'old and ugly vs. little twit' between grandfather and grandson were clearly 'trumped' by the Five Fs: The core values of Faith, Family, Friends, Fitness and Fortitude. That, along with the reminder of 86,400 seconds per day, caused this reader (as it will with others) to pause, reflect, pray, discern and decide to do everything that he/she can do, should do and must do, not IF but WHEN they are called to Carry Their Cross.

"*KEVIN COURAGEOUS: A Journey of Faith, Hope and Love* is a highly informative, extremely inspiring and sensational story that can transform peoples' lives."

Retired college administrator, writer and involved Catholic **Brian Maher** has emailed, "Maryknoll Father James Keller believed that God has given each individual a special task in life which belongs to no one else. Reflecting on the premise of *KEVIN COURAGEOUS: A Journey of Faith, Hope and Love* by Mary Ann and Chuck Mansfield, this sentiment rings loud and clear. Mixing facts, reactions, anticipations, and fears, the Mansfields describe how a sudden and life-threatening incident to their grandson Kevin sparked an overpowering response from many of those whose lives the extended Mansfield family had touched during 75 years of being there for others. Heartfelt and sincere, this tome describes the unique role Kevin will play in the reader's life, and is a reminder of how each of us, in whatever way we can, is able to help someone in need. The best part? The saga is ongoing, and, with the same determination, support, and continued prayers warmly described on each page, there will be a very happy ending to this incredible story of a young man with, indeed, a special task in life."

Acclaim for Chuck Mansfield's Fourth Book
LEADERSHIP: In Action, Thought and Word

Of the book **Lucine Marous** has written, "In this anthology Mansfield has compiled a list of dynamic contributors, some with names well-known and others whose thought and words will be new to his audience, and including topics that promise to engage their interest from the outstanding personal testimonials to the observations on the philosophy of leadership through different disciplines. More, readers of his previous books will recognize the standard of excellence they have come to know they can expect. It should be added that every insight to be gleaned from this reading has been approved by an author whose own leadership qualities were first recognized by his community when he was a secondary school student. Bravo."

Retired registered nurse **Kay Payne** has emailed, "How fitting for Chuck Mansfield to write a book on leadership. After having read his first three books and getting to know Chuck, he has been a great and accomplished leader throughout his life. His latest book on leadership is as excellent as the others. This book includes a collection of essays from Chuck and his friends and colleagues from all walks of life. A common theme that I see in many of the writings is the effectiveness of servant leadership as modeled by our Lord Jesus Christ. I highly recommend this superb book and I think Chuck has another winner!"

Retired senior bank executive, adjunct professor at Northeastern University in its Finance and Leadership programs and holder of a similar position at Harvard University, **Kevin J. McCullagh** has accorded the book five stars on www.amazon.com as follows: "What a great collection of insights into Leadership from individuals having diverse backgrounds and experiences. This book provides reflections from so many individuals who are or were corporate and military leaders and offers highly useful insights into leadership. This book can be a great resource for those early in their chosen field as well as parents looking for paths for successful outcomes. The multitude of authors, which is the strength of the book, share their views and opinions on how leadership is defined and pursued. While there is no one path for leadership success, the insights of the various authors help break the trail for your own leadership achievement."

Dr. Dennis C. Golden, President Emeritus of Fontbonne University and a former Marine Corps officer, has written, "Chuck Mansfield's book titled *LEADERSHIP: In Action, Thought and Word* is a sterling presentation of the core values of courage, commitment, command presence and more. He has gone broad and deep on the style, substance and essence of leadership. Well done!"

Kevin Loughlin, M.D., M.B.A., has written, "The age old question is whether leaders are born or made. The answer is probably both. When one analyzes the cause of failure in almost any aspect of society, ineffective leadership invariably plays a role.

"Chuck Mansfield is a born leader. From student council president to Marine platoon leader to business executive, he has honed his leadership skills throughout a lifetime.

"There are many books on leadership, but Chuck's book is unique. Not only has he included multiple authors, but authors from multiple backgrounds. Leadership lessons are transferable. What is true in business is true in the military, what is true in the military is true in education, what is true in education is true in medicine and so on. This is a book to be read from cover to cover or in segments. It should be read and reread."

According to **Brother Lawrence W. Syriac, S.M.**, of Chaminade High School (Mineola, N.Y.), "After reading this much anticipated work on leadership, I found myself listing the most important qualities of leadership consistently found in these inspiring reflections. Some of the characteristics mentioned frequently in the various chapters are: integrity, humility, accountability, strategic vision, strong communication and interpersonal skills, the ability to sweat the small stuff and the ability to inspire.

"After fifty-eight years in various leadership positions and trying to mold leaders out of my students, I wish I could say that I have all or even most of these qualities; however, there is always hope.

"Some of the other ideas that resonated with me were: We all love positive people, leadership is not for everyone, and leadership is not power; it is persuasion. Reading Martin Luther King's ten commandments was most inspiring.

"Finally, as one who has spent most of his life at Chaminade and with Chaminade people, we can never forget our guiding principle, 'Doing the right thing at the right time because it is the right thing to do, regardless of who is watching.'"

Former Marine Corps combat helicopter pilot and Vietnam War veteran **Bain D. Slack** has written, "In his latest book, *LEADERSHIP: In Action, Thought and Word*, Chuck Mansfield has chosen a subject in which he has unmatched expertise. He was himself a leader in his school years in both academic and athletic excellence. More importantly, as a U.S. Marine Corps officer in combat during the Viet Nam War, he earned the respect of the troops under his command. After military service, Chuck became a leader in the national and international business world in the financial industry. With this book he has demonstrated the greatest leadership trait of all by helping others solve their problems.

"Read this book. I guarantee that you will enjoy it and profit from what you learn from it."

Former U.S. Air Force pilot, Vietnam veteran and business executive **Valentine W. Riordan II** has written, "Mansfield's latest and greatest book on *LEADERSHIP* looks like it's going to be another winner and a great read. I really enjoyed the approach he has taken in his earlier books of grabbing an important topic and reaching out to his vast network of friends and colleagues to draw on their extensive experience and expertise to define their perspective on the chosen subject. Mansfield's *BITS AND PIECES: Stories to Soothe the Soul or Raise the Hackles* and *VIETNAM: Remembrances of a War* are two great examples of getting the real story from folks who've been there, done that. I suspect that his *LEADERSHIP* book will deliver the same experience."

Of the book the late CPA and essayist **John M. McIntyre** has written, "The book has been enjoyable and informative. Mansfield has got a well-rounded and diverse group of contributors."

Retired CEO **James C. Norwood, Jr.** has emailed, "Four hours Saturday and three today of wonderment….great job!"

Retired CEO and author **Raymond P. Zambuto** has written, "Thank you again for the opportunity to participate in the messaging of this terrific work. I am honored to find my name in the list of distinguished contributors, and particularly proud to be following the essay by Admiral McRaven. I read the book one essay a night and was so thoroughly impressed with the consistent quality of the presentations."

Acclaim for Chuck Mansfield's Third Book
VIETNAM: Remembrances of a War

Lucine Marous has emailed, "The contribution from Mansfield's friend and fellow Marine Frank Teague strengthens the story he tells in this new book. It seems that there is a substantial population of us whose knowledge of the Vietnam War was formed by journalists and by the propaganda promoted by and for the benefit of those whose agenda was at issue. It is very moving to read the stories of men like Nelson DeMille, Phillip Jennings, Val Riordan, General Brady, Dennis Golden, Mark Moyar and the author, speaking knowledgeably and from personal first-hand experience. That so many would be willing to re-create that very difficult time in their lives to make known to us the realities of their situation is, in itself, revelatory. Surely, there will be many others like myself who are grateful to Mansfield for his willingness to share his often painful life experiences and those of others in regard to the war in Southeast Asia."

Thomas P. Kiley, Jr. has emailed that "Mansfield's book is an outstanding contribution to our literature about Vietnam and provides a needed corrective to the more tendentious elements and relativism of the PBS Burns-Novick documentary. It is perhaps the truest, most beautiful and compelling that I have ever read. Each selection is a revelation and a gift."

Dr. Dennis C. Golden, President Emeritus of Fontbonne University and Vietnam-era Marine Corps officer, has written, "Just say 'NAM' and you will always evoke strong and usually differing emotions about what happened and why in Southeast Asia between 1963 and 1973.

"The answers to the questions about what really happened 'in country' can now be found in the book written, organized and edited by U.S. Marine combat veteran Chuck Mansfield, entitled *VIETNAM: Remembrances of a War.*

"In *Remembrances* you will learn about the six crucial combat mistakes that were superimposed on the combat field commanders. These mistakes put our troops in imminent and unnecessary danger. This was compounded by the fact that there was never a Congressional Declaration of War. Consequently, our troops fought with unquestioned valor but with no chance of victory and many say this was a tragedy; others say it was calculated treason.

"Mansfield and others say the lesson to be learned is never again engage in armed conflict unless we intend to win. The question for you to decide is have we learned that lesson? And if not, what are you going to do about it?"

Former Marine Corps combat helicopter pilot and Vietnam War veteran **Bain D. Slack** has written, "Chuck Mansfield has done us a much needed service in writing and compiling these many opinions and memories of a wide variety of people in his latest book, *VIETNAM: Remembrances of a War*.

"After fifty long years of biased anti-American and anti-American-military propaganda pieces, written and spoken by so-called journalists, entertainers, filmmakers and politicians, this book offers a refreshing counterpoint by other people, many of whom actually fought in the war, and who have a different opinion of why and how the U.S. entered the war and attempted to save South Vietnam from being taken over by a savage and cruel communist regime that proceeded to imprison, torture and oppress its people. It is a terrific book."

Of the book former Marine Corps officer and decorated Vietnam War veteran **George Selcke** has written that "Mansfield's eloquence stands on its own merits."

Former U.S. Marine, business strategist and author **Hank Boerner** has written: "This is a book that every American should read to understand the enormous contributions of the U.S. Marine Corps in protecting our personal and collective freedoms. The range of stories well told is amazing and encouraging; we hear the first-hand stories of so many patriots defending our freedom and the freedom of many people around the world. The variety of stories and shared perspectives makes this volume one that Americans of all generations should read. Thanks to Mansfield for a great work!"

Former U.S. Army soldier and decorated Vietnam War veteran **James J. Kiley** has emailed, "What a wonderful cover. The depiction of the Vietnam Service Medal jumps from the page and says it all. And the content did not disappoint.

"I have always known that the experiences of Vietnam veterans were as diverse as those who served there. From the rice paddies of the Mekong Delta to the northernmost reaches of Quang Tri Province along the DMZ, our experiences were shaped by where we served, how we served, and with whom we served. Whether sleeping on a cot in DaNang or on the ground in the Ashau Valley, we all shared the same fears. And hopes. The omnipresent threat of 'incoming' was known to all those serving in country. Lives could be lost anywhere at any time. ... We were all targets. But regardless of how or where they served, they still share a common bond – they served. And that's what sets us apart from those who didn't. We served.

"Thank you for including my 'poem' in your book. I am honored to be included with the many who have shared their thoughts and memories with you. And thank you for undertaking this task. For me personally, you have provided the impetus needed to unburden myself from thoughts that have haunted me through the years – but kept buried within. And for that I will be forever grateful."

According to former Marine and Vietnam-era veteran **Andy Chambliss**, "The book is well laid out, articles/commentaries are well done, interesting, not provocative (at least for me), REAL history. I am thoroughly enjoying the reading. Those who have written articles in it may be known to many veterans. I encourage all to buy a copy and read perspectives of the war from those who were there, in country and in the inner circle of what today is called the swamp. All branches are touched. Semper Fi."

Frank Rush has written, "I just finished reading Mansfield's book on Vietnam ... I really enjoyed the part where Jane Fonda was taken to task. My father, who was a WW II veteran Regular Army Pacific Theatre, was irate with her behavior and would have loved the payback she received.

"The book certainly cleared up a number of misconceptions about Vietnam and Ken Burns' documentary. I am also a product of a Catholic education from grade school through college and we share many of the same values, which today are unfortunately lacking.

"I thank the author for the great read and introducing to me these brave men who fought and sacrificed so much for their country. And I thank him for his service."

Retired executive **Marjorie P. Smuts** has emailed, "Thanks so much for sending me a copy of your latest book. I had a chance yesterday to read several of the narratives and many are truly heroic. What a good idea to let men and women tell their own stories and share their experiences in their own words. It was a noble mission on your part to make that happen."

Executive recruiter **Michael Rush** has written, "Just finished *VIETNAM: Remembrances of a War* and wished to send along a big 'Well Done.' Brought to life a period of time when we were young, happy and somewhat naïve. It was good to hear the voices of real heroes who put themselves in harm's way for their country. A tribute to American warriors, especially the US Marine Corps."

Marine Corps aviator and Vietnam War veteran **Colonel Robert "Bob" Mitchell, USMC (Ret.)** has commented, "I received the VIETNAM book that Bain Slack sent and I am enjoying reading it. It sure is bringing back many memories from those days of 50 years ago. I thank him so much for thinking of me and sending it. His friend Chuck Mansfield is a wonderful writer who has really brought Vietnam experiences to light. A book well done."

New York textile Production Manager **Joseph M. Sullivan** has reported, "I am enjoying Mansfield's newest book on Vietnam; it gives great insight into the heartbeat of great people who have opened their souls to their Vietnam feelings and experiences."

Former Air Force pilot and Vietnam War veteran **Jeffrey Smith** has emailed, "Mansfield has done a great service by bringing the voices of those who proudly served, as counterpoint to the false narrative of the left."

Acclaim for Chuck Mansfield's Second Book
BITS AND PIECES: Stories to Soothe
the Soul or Raise the Hackles

Lucine Marous has written, "From the warmth of the tributes honoring family and friends to the sharpness of the political comments in the vignettes chosen to be a part of the book there is ample evidence presented to support and fulfill the challenges of its title. Additionally, 'Things That Have Paid Off for Me in My Life' reveals the strength of character of the author which undoubtedly contributes to making the book so interesting to peruse. As every reader will learn, there is much here to warm the cockles of the heart."

Linda Giarraputo Jeans has emailed, "Powerful with no guessing where Mansfield stands. I have friends who would probably burn it, but I know more who will be cheering when they read this."

Former Marine Corps combat helicopter pilot and Vietnam War veteran **Bain D. Slack** has written, "Chuck Mansfield has proven before that he is a terrific author, editor, critic and philosopher. But he has outdone himself with *BITS AND PIECES*. When I read this book I laughed out loud at its humorous bits and I cried like a baby over its heart-breaking, gut-wrenching tragic pieces. This book gives us much needed relief from the idiotic, politically correct drivel that we have been inundated with for the past decade or so. It is a much longed-for return to that old fashioned American common sense. Every bit and every piece is dead-on accurate, right on target, right in the center of the bull's eye. I loved every word of this book. We need Mansfield's words in an era of such pathetic political correctness and so many lies by the left wing media and politicians." Subsequently, Mr. Slack posted the following at www.amazon.com: "Outstanding!! Chuck Mansfield is the brightest light in today's publishing world. This book is a treasure. I enjoyed every Bit and Piece in it. I highly recommend it."

Anne Groh has emailed that "I believe Mansfield's new book is going to be a very accurate telling of the current history of our times."

On www.amazon.com **Raymond P. Zambuto** responded to its request for an evaluation as follows: "A superb collection of thought provoking articles, personal and sometimes prophetic observations of the American scene, presented in typical Mansfield no-nonsense fashion. A refreshing read. Approach each article with an open mind, read it, and then decide if it 'soothes' or 'raises hackles.'"

Retired educator **Lee Jeans** has emailed, "I just finished Mansfield's book and am amazed at its content and relevance to today's society. He hit it right on the target of what we are going through today with the divisiveness within our politics and our society. Everything from his upbringing, Chaminade, colleges and his life ongoing was wonderfully covered. He has the ability to put into words, as well as other people's words, his beliefs that he acquired from his past. The research needed to obtain all the articles and speeches he put together in the book just shows how much he cares about our wonderful United States of America. I thank him for sending 'Bits and Pieces' to my wife Linda. As the cover shows, he put the puzzle together wonderfully."

Former U.S. Air Force officer and gastroenterologist **Dr. Denis M. Murphy** has emailed, "Finally read the preface to your book. If the book is anything like the preface, it's going to be a gang buster! I shared that with Maureen and she agrees."

U.S. Navy veteran and retired CEO **James C. Norwood, Jr.** has written, "I found Mansfield's new book well written, informative and I think he has a winner. I'm enjoying a beautiful summer Sunday reading from his work and must express how much I cherish being friends with a true modern day scholar."

Former U.S. Air Force pilot, Vietnam veteran and business executive **Valentine W. Riordan II** has written, "Love the mix of writings.

I suspect that it will turn out to be great follow up to Dr. Charles Krauthammer's "Things that Matter"! … I'm further into it today and thoroughly enjoying it. With this type of book, I love the 'to the pointness' of the articles, letters and commentary. Fast paced and you can read it for two hours or ten minutes and still come away satisfied. Just finished reading 'Burial at Sea' in *BITS AND PIECES*. I had to stop twice as tears welled up in my eyes. Just so touching. I lost several friends in Nam and my college roommate, a Marine, was killed thirty days in country. Thanks for this great book."

Brother Lawrence W. Syriac, S.M., of Chaminade High School (Mineola, N.Y.) has called the book "a great read and at times funny. I like the way it is sectioned off so you can read at several sittings."

J. Michael Reisert has emailed, "I have the book and what I've read so far is truly enjoyable. What strikes me is the sensible replies against some very disturbing positions of some people. We need to become more outspoken for the sake of our silent majority."

Former U.S. Air Force combat fighter pilot, Vietnam War veteran and career American Airlines pilot **George A. Krumenacker** has emailed, "I read a good chunk of Mansfield's manuscript and I find his compilation of vignettes a combination of common-sense conservative with a touch of whimsy and humor. Riveting throughout and fun and easy to read. Very enjoyable."

Former Marine Corps captain and New Jersey judge **Edwin R. Matthews** has written, "I am reading '*BITS AND PIECES*.' I find it fascinating particularly Mansfield's extremely well thought out and well written screw-you letters."

Earl S. Montgomery has written that "The book is full of wisdom and common sense; seems just what the world lacks today."

New York City production manager **Joseph M. Sullivan** has emailed, "I am sitting home first morning of the New Year continuing reading *BITS AND PIECES*. I am enjoying the book and find myself sharing with my son Shane many bits and pieces on life's journey, and Mansfield has provided many examples of an officer and a gentleman with the way he has conducted his life. I also appreciate his strong Catholic faith and will continue to read with pleasure."

Basketball coach **Michael Bowser** has written, "I asked for and received Mansfield's book for Christmas. Reading and enjoying it. Easy to pick up and put down as I travel on buses with my basketball team. Great job!"

Acclaim for Chuck Mansfield's First Book
NO KIDS, NO MONEY AND A CHEVY:
A Politically Incorrect Memoir

Award-winning novelist and essayist **Cynthia Ozick** has written, "Chuck Mansfield is a first-rate writer of wit, charm, and passion, who applies a clarifying integrity to whatever subject his fine mind alights on. Having been schooled in excellence, he holds it as his lifelong standard; and he is, besides, an embodiment of everything that is meant by the term American Hero – courtly, brave, generous, and in love with family, faith, and country. To read his memoir is to rejoice in the warm presence of human devotion and intellect."

Linda Giarraputo Jeans has written, "His book is more than his story; it is a tribute to manhood. He sets such a commendable example to his children and grandchildren that I wish it were the example set for all children. Our society so desperately needs true men, men who are brave, honest, intelligent, responsible, respectful, loyal and loving. I thank him for being a man I want to call my friend."

Former Marine Corps combat helicopter pilot and Vietnam War veteran **Bain D. Slack** has posted the following review on Amazon. com: "This is a great book written by a great man. He tells a story of a true American citizen lived like an American man ought to live his life and his story is the kind of life that made the USA the greatest nation in the history of the world. This nation was built on the backs of men like Chuck Mansfield. He is not only a terrific writer, he is a true American Hero. Chuck Mansfield, a fellow Marine Officer, saved my life. Yes, literally saved my life, by taking his own time and energy and causing the Veterans Administration to grant me the benefits that I earned on the battlefields in Viet Nam, many years ago. Chuck Mansfield is my hero. And I will try to get him to write more great books like this one."

The late retired corporate executive, U.S. Air Force Vietnam veteran and author **Francis X. Biasi, Jr.** has written on Amazon.com that "Mr.

Mansfield stirred in me a renewed passion for personal responsibility and integrity. While there is much in this book to be taken to heart, it was in the profiles of numerous remarkable people that both intrigued and challenged me. The character, heroism, and values of so many 'mainstream' individuals are rarely as powerfully and articulately chronicled in one place. Don't rush the reading; enjoy it slowly like a good wine."

Retired Marriott International executive **William T. Walsh** has emailed, "The book was awesome! The stories told made me think about my Dad and how he returned from war with nothing and built a great life with my mother for my sisters, brother and me. I could not help but think as I was reading the book that how much better a place the world would be if we had more Chuck Mansfields. I'm not just talking about his ideals of Catholic faith, but how hard work, 'sticktoitiveness' (as Mom used to say), and finding the good in people can go a long way. I thank him for writing such a wonderful book that will certainly inspire all that read it. It proudly sits on my desk at work."

Linda Satterlee, widow of a fallen Marine, has written, "It's time for me to take a moment and thank him for what he wrote in his book. His gift will remain in my heart and in my hands for the rest of my life. The way he recalls his family and friends is amazing and it's the best book I have read this year. The best. Thanks for this wonderful book, I am ever so grateful to read it and will read it again when retired."

New York textile Production Manager **Joseph M. Sullivan** has reported, "I finished reading Mansfield's book and enjoyed it immensely. I wish the book did not end."

Lieutenant General **Arthur Blades**, USMC (Ret.) has written, "Received Mansfield's book last week and have thoroughly enjoyed reading it… His attention to detail and presentation creates some very vivid images and certainly is a rich legacy that he has left his children."

Lieutenant General **Frederick N. McCorkle**, USMC (Ret.) has called the author "a Warrior, Marine, and Great American. Thank you for all that you have contributed to our Corps and Country!"

Alison Territ has written, "I enjoyed it cover to cover and was struck time and time again how well it captured the essence that is Mansfield – his passion, dedication and integrity for all things meaningful. What a tremendously delightful treasure!"

Major General **Matthew P. Caulfield**, USMC (Ret.) has called the book "a great credit to Mansfield and the Marine Corps… The Marines should be grateful for the use of its Eagle, Globe and Anchor emblem on the cover of a book which speaks volumes of the values which the Corps stands for and the Corps' justifiable pride that a person of his caliber is a former Marine."

Former U.S. Air Force combat fighter pilot, Vietnam War veteran and career American Airlines pilot **George A. Krumenacker** has written: "I never knew you that well before but I know you now. The book was fabulous. I've not found too many people in my life that think the way I do, but you apparently are part of that select group. Nice job on the book. I concur with 100% of your assessments and observations of life. … I could really relate…cover to cover."

Marine Corps rifle platoon commander Second Lieutenant **James F. Colvin** has written from Ramadi, Iraq, "I stayed up to six in the morning reading Mansfield's book the first night I opened it. I find his story extremely inspirational and one I can relate to."

Patrick Donnelly, executive vice president and general counsel for a leading satellite radio company, has written: *NO KIDS, NO MONEY AND A CHEVY* arrived on Wednesday afternoon and I could not put it down. I finished at 1:00 a.m. on Saturday. While I have always been impressed by Mansfield's faith, courage and convictions, the book brought all those qualities more clearly into focus. I especially enjoyed the chapters on the Marine Corps and Vietnam."

Physician **Vincent P. Garbitelli** states, "It is heartening to see the strength of Mansfield's Catholic faith carry him through such difficult times as his experience during the Vietnam War… I believe as he does that we must speak out against the crumbling morality in this country and the world."

Pastor **William R. Masciangelo**, a retired Marine Corps Lieutenant Colonel and a Vietnam War veteran, has written: "The book is fantastic and powerful…most fascinating for me…can't put it down… It allows me to relive my own path growing up in New Jersey…with friends, neighbors, teachers and school. Bless him for writing…it is an era gone by for sure…Great book."

CEO, business owner, former Marine and Vietnam War veteran **Donald J. Steinert** says, "I was most impressed with the way I am able to relate to Mansfield's book as a former Marine Vietnam veteran."

Manager-Event Coordinator **Kathy Fives** says, "I so enjoyed this book from start to finish and didn't want it to end; maybe Mansfield could write another one. I felt…a part of his family and friends, growing up right beside him. I could feel the warmth and goodness of everyone he described so well. I really admire him, that he could put all these wonderful memories into such a beautiful and inspiring book. I thank him from the bottom of my heart."

New York attorney **Paul G. Burns** has written, "Mansfield's work shares a problem common to each and every book that I totally and thoroughly enjoyed reading: it had a last page. …an outstanding read!!"

Risk management executive and author **Michael R. Granito** has written, "This is an extraordinary work that will be fondly and proudly remembered by Mansfield's family and friends for generations to come."

According to retired English professor and writer **Robert P. Meikle**, "everything in the book is the unfiltered Mansfield: the impeccable use of language, the meticulous attention to detail, the total recall of dates… Some are more successful than others when it comes to taking a really honest look at themselves. The trick is to translate that self-awareness onto the written page. It is that translation that Mansfield does so successfully. This is a guy who not only has had a good life, but who APPRECIATES all that he has had in it, especially when it comes to family and friends. That's an important distinction for that unknown reader to pick up on."

Former Marine Corps officer and Vietnam veteran **John Ewing** says "Mansfield's book would be a bargain at twice the price and has thus far brought back a lot of memories, most of them good. Mansfield also says very eloquently many things that should be said, and read. I congratulate him for a splendid effort."

Former reporter and New Jersey Senate presidential communications director **James J. Manion** has emailed, "Just finished your memoir… great read…and what a family treasure to have on the Mansfield book shelves from Mineola to North Carolina to London."

Maureen Monteleone has written, "What a gift Mansfield has given his children and grandchildren. What a life he and his wife have had living in different countries. I can't tell you how much the book has taught me and how I agree with all the author's opinions. I am in awe of him for writing such an interesting and well written book."

Cardiologist **Daniel R. Landolphi** declared that "Calling it a 'book' does not do it justice. Had I not worked a long day yesterday, I may have finished it in one sitting. I thank Mansfield for sharing his faith, knowledge, wisdom, patriotism, and love of family and Chaminade High School with me. I cannot help but feel that I will be a better person after reading his memoir. It should be required reading at Chaminade.

I'm glad that it's a hard covered book – it must last after it is read by my wife, parents, brothers, and children!"

Former U.S. Air Force pilot, Vietnam veteran and business executive **Valentine W. Riordan II** has written, "WOW. What an enjoyable read and truly a trip down memory lane. So many parallels and images to my own growing up experiences. Remarkable all the places and names Mansfield was able to recall… I also applaud his various and courageous positions on life in America and the loss of our moral compass. I was also taken by the clear love and enjoyment he's had through and with his family."

Of the book **Bernice Healy** has commented, "My first impression was of nostalgic warmth and tenderness. Mansfield has done a really good thing for his family… It's what all of us secretly think about, chapters written for our children and those we love, as well as to touch others. We want someone to know about what's important to us and perhaps, ultimately, to them."

According to retired Marine Corps colonel and Vietnam War veteran **Joaquin Gracida**, "I have also enjoyed Mansfield's book. Having been raised in Mexico and not experiencing the American way of life until I was 18 years old when I enlisted in the Corps, the book has been enjoyable when I look at the similarities and differences of our lives. Sometimes I wish I could have his skills to leave something that meaningful for my children. With great admiration and respect, Semper Fidelis, Joaquin."

Landscape architect **Elizabeth "Puffy" Meikle** has written, "I was wondering if I'd find a new Chuck – one who … might have been hard to recognize from the written word. But no, he was very much present in the pages as the Chuck I had known and grown to love and respect. As I read … I felt as though we might have been having a conversation by his pool on a summer's afternoon or having one last drink before ending the night on any number of occasions over the last thirty-odd years."

According to former Marine and corporate communications and governance expert **Henry (Hank) Boerner**, "I stand in great admiration for all that Mansfield has accomplished. His book is a terrific read and really speaks to the opportunities afforded us in this great country. The two defining experiences in his life, Chaminade High School and the Marine Corps, are well described. ... I feel like I am looking over his shoulder as he rolls out the scenes of his life. Flashbacks, great stories. He has a way with words."

Fran Greiner, friend of a Marine killed in Vietnam, has written, "I have read 'The Vietnam Era' over and over and each time came away in tears. Such a terrible time, such wonderful young men."

ConEdison of New York specialist **Patrick Boland** has written, "Mansfield's book ... was a pleasure and I was deeply moved. I thank him for his service... He set a great example and I hope that one day I can be half the man that he is. I thank him for telling his story."

KEVIN COURAGEOUS

A JOURNEY OF FAITH, HOPE AND LOVE

Mary Ann and Chuck Mansfield

Copyright © 2020 by Mary Ann and Chuck Mansfield.

Library of Congress Control Number:		2020905422
ISBN:	Hardcover	978-1-7960-9496-1
	Softcover	978-1-7960-9495-4
	eBook	978-1-7960-9494-7

All rights reserved. No part of this book may be reproduced or transmitted in any form or by any means, electronic or mechanical, including photocopying, recording, or by any information storage and retrieval system, without permission in writing from the copyright owner.

Any people depicted in stock imagery provided by Getty Images are models, and such images are being used for illustrative purposes only.
Certain stock imagery © Getty Images.

Taken on March 2, 2018, just one week after Kevin Sean Mansfield was hospitalized, this book's cover photo is entitled "All Hands in for Kevin" (#allhandsin4kevin) and depicts the hands of his parents and siblings touching his hands while he was comatose. The photograph is courtesy of Dawn Mansfield and published with her permission.

The image of a butterfly by Clker-Free-Vector-Images from Pixabay appears on the cover and frequently in the body of this work. According to www.gardenswithwings.com, "The Christian religion sees the butterfly as a symbol of resurrection. Around the world, people view the butterfly as representing endurance, change, hope, and life." Accordingly, the authors believe the butterfly's image is well suited to Kevin Sean Mansfield and the message herein.

Scripture is taken from the World English Bible.

The photograph of the authors on the rear dust jacket flap is courtesy of Elizabeth Boyce and published with her permission.

Print information available on the last page.

Rev. date: 03/26/2020

To order additional copies of this book, contact:
Xlibris
1-888-795-4274
www.Xlibris.com
Orders@Xlibris.com
809986

CONTENTS

Foreword
By Dawn Chiaramonte Mansfield xxxi

Preface xxxiii
Dedication xxxviii
Other Writings By Mary Ann Mansfield................................. xxxix
Other Writings By Chuck Mansfield xl
Acknowledgements xliii

The First Night
By Dawn Chiaramonte Mansfield 1

Kevin, My Son: A Father's Perspective
By Charles F. Mansfield III 8

We Needed To Know That Everything Would Be Okay
By Timothy Charles Mansfield 29

Little Brothers Are Worth Everything
By Marissa Hope Mansfield 33

Just In Time
By Justin Conner Mansfield 37

Mamie's Memories
By Mary Ann Mansfield 39

A Poem
By Marissa Hope Mansfield 47

Kevin
By Kathryn Mary Mansfield 49

Anem Not Amen
By Chuck Mansfield..51

Have I Lost My Mind?
By Dawn Chiaramonte Mansfield
With Illustrations by Jane Tronco...58

Messages From An Amputee Friend
By Brian Maher..70

A Month Of Emails
By Mary Ann and Chuck Mansfield 77

My First Hospital Visit With Kevin
By Chuck Mansfield... 102

Kevin Sean Mansfield, R.O.A.
By Chuck Mansfield... 104

Kevin And Genesius
By Chuck Mansfield... 107

A Tragic Accident At Age 18 And A Great Life Thereafter
By Jack Stillwaggon 110

Kevin's Giggles
By Kevin Sean and Dawn Chiaramonte Mansfield 114

Crisis And The Five Fs
By Chuck Mansfield... 124

Alex And Jean Trebek Receive Fordham Founder's Award
By Tom Stoelker... 126

The Magic Bank Account
By Paul "Bear" Bryant 130

Why Women Cry
Author Unknown 133

They Never Gave Up!
By Doyce G. Payne 135

Our Village
By Dawn Chiaramonte Mansfield and Mary Ann Mansfield 137

Gratitude for GoFundMe and Other Donors 140

A Mother's Musings
By Dawn Chiaramonte Mansfield 143

Two Years After The Worst Day
By Dawn Chiaramonte Mansfield 147

"Invictus"
By William Ernest Henley 150

Here And Now: In His Own Words
By Kevin Sean Mansfield Assisted by His Dad 152

Epilogue 159
About The Authors 161

FOREWORD

By Dawn Chiaramonte Mansfield

Dawn is Kevin's mother. She penned the following journal entry on February 23, 2019, exactly one year after she found him unconscious and unresponsive.

Life as we knew it changed one year ago today! At this time, last year, there was so much unknown. A lot has changed in this year. Kevin has made some great strides. His strength is amazing. He needs a hand when going down wide or deep staircases but otherwise his balance is good. His double vision is almost all gone. Today was actually the first day he was walking around some without his glasses on. His short-term memory is still an issue although it has improved some. Our biggest obstacle is the tremors in his hands. They seem to have gotten worse over the past few months. Kevin has started back with Occupational Therapy to work with this issue. His doctors have been experimenting with different medications to see what helps the tremors but so far they have been no help. We are scheduled to go see a new doctor who specializes in movement disorders.

Since Kevin graduated [from high school] at the end of 2018, we are in the first steps of Vocational Rehabilitation. This is a program that will help Kevin either find and keep a job or guide him through his educational experience.

Today, one year later, I am eternally grateful...for Kevin being here with us...for my family who has gotten through this stronger... for our village whom we will never be able to thank enough...and most importantly, I am so grateful that God has given me the chance to spend more time with my son.

Walk with the dreamers, the believers, the courageous, the cheerful, the planners, the doers, the successful people with their heads in the clouds and their feet on the ground. Let their spirit ignite a fire within you to leave this world better than when you found it.

– Wilferd Peterson

Kevin as a toddler.
(Photograph courtesy of Dawn Mansfield and republished with her permission.)

PREFACE

I can think of no better way to instill hopelessness and fear in a young person than to tell him he is a victim, powerless to change his circumstance.

— Robert L. Woodson

It was late on the afternoon of Friday, February 23, 2018, when our daughter-in-law, Dawn Chiaramonte Mansfield, telephoned with shocking and tragic news.

A few hours earlier, she had returned to their Charlotte, North Carolina, home to drive son Kevin, then 18, to a doctor's appointment. He had been home from school for two days with an as yet unknown illness subsequently diagnosed as the flu. Kevin's sister, Marissa, was home with him at the time and, unaware of any problem, told her mother that Kevin was napping.

Dawn climbed the staircase to Kevin's bedroom to awaken him. What she found was her young son, not asleep but unconscious and unresponsive. Immediately she called 911, and emergency medical personnel arrived promptly to take Kevin to the hospital emergency room.

In the ER doctors and nurses worked feverishly to determine what had afflicted Kevin but they and Kevin's parents, even at the time of Dawn's telephone call to her mother-in-law, did not know the cause of Kevin's possibly life-threatening condition. Kevin remained unconscious and unresponsive. Indeed, he lay comatose for the next seven days.

While it was concluded after a few days that Kevin was suffering initially from a strain of influenza, this flu had morphed into a case of encephalitis, a potentially deadly swelling or inflammation of the brain. We learned belatedly that Kevin's was only the second case of flu-induced encephalitis reported in the United States! Talk about being dealt a bad hand.

What followed was a week from hell. The medical personnel attending to Kevin were not confident that he would live and forthrightly communicated their views to Dawn and Chas, her husband and Kevin's Dad. It was day-to-day and minute-to-minute with Kevin's mother never leaving his hospital room. There was sound reason for her staying close: Kevin was totally unable to press his red help button. Dawn slept in her son's room every night for some six weeks, leaving the hospital only for short periods to shower and change clothes. Her dedication and loving care for her Kevin were and are epic and heroic.

What ensued for the following several months were daily updates, almost always from Dawn, about Kevin's condition and prognosis. Because of the doubts concerning this young man's survivability, people prayed. Enter the prayer brigade, aka the prayer warriors.

Mary Mansfield, Kevin's paternal great-grandmother, always believed unswervingly in "the power of prayer." She raised her six children in a prayerful Christian home, starting at the tenderest of ages. Nightly prayers said on one's knees were de rigueur. Well, family and friends all over the country, nay, the world, were enlisted to pray for Kevin's recovery, despite the gloomy outlook. Moreover, entire religious orders, such as the Discalced Carmelites and the Society of Mary (Marianists), transmitted prayer orders for Kevin to all their members around the globe! It was magnificent and deeply gratifying to all of us, and we owe our profound gratitude to all, which we offer here and in the dedication of this work on the page following this preface.

About twenty-three months ago, with his mother by his side, Kevin, still in his hospital bed, opened his eyes and emerged from the coma. He could not yet speak or stand or walk or take care of any of his personal needs. He had to be fed, washed and assisted to, in and from the bathroom. Despite his six-foot frame and eighteen years, this handsome young man faced all the challenges of a newborn. It was daunting for him and all who know and love him. We were reminded at this time of the words of Marie Francois Xavier Bichat written in 1800, "Life is the totality of those functions which resist death." Quite miraculously, we believe, Kevin resisted death and we give thanks to the Lord for sparing him and giving him renewed life.

When Mame traveled to Charlotte to visit with Kevin in his hospital room, he had regained speaking ability. While his speech was somewhat impaired, he was still fully comprehensible and articulate. He also has retained his extraordinary sense of humor. For example, a lady friend visited with Kevin, told him she knew his grandmother and was also from New York. When she stated that she was a Mets fan, Kevin declared, "That's too bad; they suck." The woman then replied, "They're actually doing better." Without hesitation, Kevin inquired, "How long was I in a coma?" Check mark in the sense-of-humor box.

Several months after he was stricken, Kevin and his family made their regular summer trip to Westhampton Beach, New York, to visit us grandparents. Kevin's left eye had been a severe casualty of the brain damage he sustained. (Thankfully, his right eye was unaffected.) In Charlotte, Kevin and his parents were counseled that his left eye would likely never improve and that an eye patch would be appropriate going forward. Shortly afterward, a decision was made to seek a second opinion, and, thanks to our great friend, Chuck's mother's "third son," Dr. Denis Murphy, an appointment was made with Dr. Floyd Warren, a leading neuro-ophthalmologist based in Manhattan. Dr. Warren examined and interviewed Kevin for about 90 minutes, after which he announced that Kevin's weakened eye was not only salvageable but may correct itself over time. By January of 2019, just seven months after Kevin's consultation with Dr. Warren and less than a year after he was afflicted, nearly normal vision had returned to Kevin's left eye. Another answer to prayers and possibly another miracle!

Kevin can no longer drive a car due to a reduced reaction time and residual hand tremors. He has also been informed recently that he is "completely and permanently disabled," a finding that understandably shocked him. With this knowledge our hearts are deeply troubled but we will not cease encouraging our wonderful grandson.

Hence, the genesis of this book derives from the following email from Chuck to our son Chas on September 14, 2018:

"Yesterday Mom and I were talking about Kevin, and she encouraged me to write a book about him, his illness and the challenges for him and everyone else concerned in its aftermath. I suggested the title *KEVIN COURAGEOUS*. *[Authors' note: We subsequently added the subtitle, "A Journey of Faith, Hope and Love."]*

"Having discussed it some more yesterday and today, we agreed that such a book might be an incentive for him to work harder to attain wellness. I am excited at the prospect and believe that our family and even countless others could and would contribute their thoughts via interviews and/or writings. Obviously, Kevin's immediate family members have already written beautiful reflections about him and the awful hit he has taken and sustained at such an early and formative stage of his life. Kevin's plans and dreams before February 23, 2018, versus what he sees himself accomplishing in the wake of a horrific experience would be moving. Dawn's chronicle of his hospitalization, return to consciousness and still powerful intellect and remarkable sense of humor, as well as so many other aspects of this amazing human trauma and drama, is just one source of elements of this extraordinary tale that includes everything on the pain-to-joy spectrum. Quotations from Kevin himself are other sources of great human interest and overcoming adversity. The GoFundMe website, the myriad prayers from people worldwide and all the outpouring of support from literally thousands of people make for an uplifting and potentially heartwarming story.

"What I've written above hardly scratches the surface of all that could and should be told. The outcome, that is, in terms of a happy ending, will depend in large measure on how hard Kevin is willing to work to recover what he has so unfairly lost. Kevin himself could add a memorable dimension to his own story by keeping a journal going forward. His own contribution to his own story would be a valuable authentication and validation of a tale as yet incomplete. As the song goes, 'We've only just begun.'

"Mom and I would welcome your thoughts.

"I love you,

Dad"

And so, we share the "Kevin" stories of family, friends and strangers. They are filled with faith in the power of prayer, hope for a happy ending, and love for a courageous young man who will overcome the tragedies on his life's journey.

March 16, 2020

Kevin, age 4, as Superman in 2003.
(Photograph courtesy of Dawn Mansfield and published with her permission.)

*For all those family members, friends and
countless others around the world
who responded so magnificently with their
thoughts, prayers, encouraging words,
good wishes and financial support to the tragic
illness that befell Kevin Sean Mansfield,
our 18-year old grandson, on February 23, 2018,
and whose strong faith, hope and love
moved and strengthened us when we needed them most.*

OTHER WRITINGS BY MARY ANN MANSFIELD

The EX-Files: A Study of Exponential Decay, National Teacher Training Institute (NTTI), Math Science &Technology 1997-1998 Manual

Weaving the Web: Using Video, the Internet and the CBL with Graphing Calculator in a Pre-Calculus Classroom, Article for NTTI Newsletter, Spring 1999

Contributor to *Math Olympiad Contest Problems Volumes 2 and 3*, edited by Richard Kalman

A Primer for First Time Calculus Teachers

Out and About (Florida Sandpebble Beach Condominium newsletter)

Travels With Mame (Tale of 2013 trip to Africa published in the 2017 book *BITS AND PIECES: Stories to Soothe the Soul or Raise the Hackles*)

Contributor to Educators' Guide for Math Midway (Exhibit for the Museum of Mathematics [MOMATH])

OTHER WRITINGS BY CHUCK MANSFIELD

Books

NO KIDS, NO MONEY AND A CHEVY:
A Politically Incorrect Memoir
BITS AND PIECES: Stories to Soothe the Soul or Raise the Hackles
VIETNAM: Remembrances of a War
LEADERSHIP: In Action, Thought and Word

Poems

Time Cannot Kill
Ode to the World of Light
Vietnam Valentine: Reflections on Leaving You and Coming Home
Ode to Joy, Also Known As Mame

Essays and Letters

An Approach to Evaluating Foreign Bank Credit Risk
Another Vote for Export Trading Firms
Biography of G. Michael Hostage
Contemporary Commercial Bank Credit Policy:
Economic Rationale and Ramifications
Credit Policy and Risk Acceptability for
International Financial Institutions
The Function of Credit Analysis in a U.S. Commercial Bank

Giving the Best Its Due
It Wasn't Mere Flaw That Led to Tragedy
Legislators and Regulators Failed in 2007
Letters of Credit: Promises to Keep
Lessons from a Legend
Too Many Hats
Vietnam Memory: Acts of Good Faith
Vocations: Our Urgent Need
What Does the Tet Offensive Have to Teach Us 40 Years Later?

ACKNOWLEDGEMENTS

The authors' gratitude is owed and offered to the following, whose willingness to share their writings and/or otherwise help in the production of this work is deeply appreciated.

Laura Aquilone
Yosef Borenstein
Elizabeth Boyce
Paul "Bear" Bryant
John Devine
Fordham University
Dennis C. Golden, Ed.D.
William Ernest Henley
Jill Horbacewicz, PT, Ph.D.
Carrie Jones
Kevin's "Prayer Warriors"
Thomas P. Kiley, Jr.
Martin Luther King, Jr.
Nicole LaRosa
Heath Hardage Lee
Huey Lewis and the News
Brian Maher
Charles F. Mansfield III
Dawn Chiaramonte Mansfield
Justin Conner Mansfield
Kathryn Mary Mansfield
Kevin Sean Mansfield
Marissa Hope Mansfield
Timothy Charles Mansfield
Lucine Marous
Kevin J. McCullagh
Kait McKay

Friedrich Nietzsche
James C. Norwood, Jr.
Andrew Olsen
Cynthia Ozick
Doyce G. Payne, M.D., F.A.C.O.G.
Kay E. Payne, R.N.
Peter Shepherd
shs.touro.edu
Sly & the Family Stone
Jack Stillwaggon
The Suffolk Times
The Wall Street Journal
Tom Stoelker
George R. Sullivan
George R. Sullivan, Jr.
Jane Tronco
U.S. Center for Disease Control and Prevention
Joe Werkmeister
Robert L. Woodson
World English Bible
www.amboss.com
www.earlychurchhistory.org
www.en.wikipedia.com
www.gardenswithwings.com
www.ghr.nlm.nih.gov

www.gofundme.com
www.pixabay.com
www.rarediseases.info.nih.gov
www.reference.com
www.sciencedirect.com
www.tomstoelker.com

THE FIRST NIGHT

By Dawn Chiaramonte Mansfield

Healing comes from taking responsibility: to realize that it is you – and no one else – that creates your thoughts, your feelings, and your actions.

– Peter Shepherd

Why did I go to work? Why didn't I check on him? Why didn't I keep calling him? How long was he unresponsive? If I were with him, it wouldn't have happened! These are the thoughts that will forever be etched on my (and Marissa's) brain. People can say, "*You couldn't have prevented it.*" My response will always be, "*How do we know?*" The EMTs seemed confident that he wasn't unresponsive for long. I don't know if that were true or if they say it just to try and keep you calm. Either way, I will never be convinced. That is my child. I am supposed to protect him. I failed!

The week of February 18th was one for the record books. It started Monday; while Kevin was at work at the afterschool program, he was playing soccer with his group of children and somehow sprained his ankle. I picked him up and off we went to OrthoCarolina. There they confirmed what we already knew. They put him in a boot and said to stay off it for two weeks. The next day, he was complaining of a scratchy throat and being congested. That, with his swollen ankle, made him stay in bed all day. He figured he probably had the same crud that his Dad had.

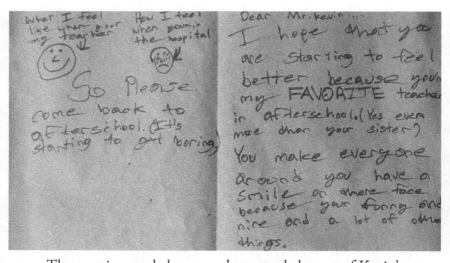

The greeting card above was homemade by one of Kevin's afterschool students. Above the happy face in the upper left, the young writer indicates with an arrow, "What I feel like when your my teacher". Next to it is a tearful face with the wording, "How I feel when your in the hospital". Beneath the two faces we read, "So please come back to afterschool. (It's starting to get boring.)" On the right side of the card are the words: "Dear Mr. Kevin… I hope that you are starting to feel better because you're my favorite teacher in afterschool. (Yes even more than your sister) You make everyone around you have a smile on there face because your funny and nice and a lot of other things." *(Image courtesy of Kevin Mansfield and published with his permission.)*

On Wednesday, Kevin was asking if there was a way he could go to work, even with the boot on. He didn't seem to have any symptoms of being sick. Then Thursday hit. Kevin hated to go to the doctor's but at 5:00 p.m. he said, *"I don't feel good and think we should make a doctor's appointment."* Of course, office hours just ended and knowing that he was asking to go to the doctor, I suggested that we go to the Minute Clinic. That was a useless trip. They stated that they didn't do flu tests anymore because they were unreliable. Kevin said that we should wait 'til tomorrow and go to the doctor. As we got home that evening, Kevin informed me that he had thrown up a couple of times that day and had a fever, but it was gone later in the day. The flu it is, I was confident. I went right on-line and made an appointment for two o'clock the next afternoon for Kevin and Marissa.

Friday, February 23, 2018, the day I would like to erase from history. Kevin is always asleep when I go to work in the morning. I checked in on him and he was doing just that. I called him once later but there was no answer. I thought he was probably downstairs without his phone or napping. Nothing out of the ordinary. Marissa was in her room most of the morning (since she wasn't feeling that well either…no flu, I was confident). My kids never check on each other during the day. It's not what kids do. It was common practice for Kevin to stay in his room and do his schoolwork before anyone saw him later in the afternoon. When I arrived home, I called up to the kids that we would be leaving in a few minutes. Marissa responded, but, at this time, I couldn't tell you what she said. I just remember that Kevin didn't answer. I went upstairs to get him moving since he was in that boot. If he was sleeping, he was going to need a few extra minutes to get himself together.

I opened the door and it was dark. My initial reaction was that he was sleeping but there was a definite eeriness to it. I called him several times getting louder each time. I went over to him and patted his face to get him to wake up. My kids are all sound sleepers. They would all sleep through the smoke alarm if it went off. Without knowing it at the time, I was probably trying to convince myself that he was in a deep sleep and a few nudges and pats would just do the trick to get him up. Not so much! A mother's worst nightmare. I didn't know if he was alive or dead. I tried to move but, for a split second, time and I were frozen. I finally got into CPR/First Aid mode for a moment and assessed the situation. I could tell that he was breathing. Check. I observed his surroundings. Nothing out of the ordinary. Check. I called for Marissa to bring me her phone. She asked if everything was ok and, trying to stay as calm as possible, I said *"I just need your phone now."* I dialed 911 and told Marissa to go get Tim in his room. That poor girl ran all over the house looking for him, until we remembered that he had driven Chas to Greensboro that morning. After she ran, what seemed like a mile, she called Chas and Tim to fill them in but was babbling. A little fact you probably don't know…if you call 911, the main number on your account gets notified. Poor Chas had no idea what had happened other than there was trouble at home. Chas has reminded me that I did call him afterwards and all I said was that Kevin was unresponsive and that I would call him back. I honestly have no idea if I ever did. I sent Marissa outside to wait for the EMTs and I called Maryanne Jackson, our neighbor and good friend, to come and be with Marissa. I wish I were able to cut myself in half at that time and be with both Marissa and Kevin, but I needed to give info to the 911 operator, and I knew Marissa couldn't be alone. Maryanne was there in a flash and I told her that they would need to go to the doctor because Marissa still needed to be seen and they could also tell the doctor what was going on.

The EMTs arrived and asked so many questions that I knew were not relevant. Was he depressed, was he on drugs, did he drink? They took his vitals and his temperature was just under 100 degrees. This is when I started thinking how long my poor son had been unresponsive. They started prepping Kevin for transport, so I went to check on Marissa. I really wanted her out of the way because they were bringing Kevin out to the ambulance and I didn't want her to see what I saw. When they transport you from point A to point B, not using a gurney, they use what looks like a tarp with handles. They moved Kevin downstairs in this tarp and placed him on the gurney outside in the garage. Another little fact…the tarp is black. When they brought Kevin out of the house, my heart sank, for one heart-wrenching second, I thought he was gone. *Second time thinking that in a matter of minutes.* I wasn't ready to have that happen again. No three strikes and you're out here. Someone needs to tell emergency services that these transport bags should NOT BE BLACK!

They put Kevin in the ambulance and asked me if I wanted to go with them or take my own car. I must have been in shock in some way because I chose to take my car so that I could drive Kevin and myself back from the hospital later. I got in my car, started following the ambulance to Novant Presbyterian Hospital and I remember getting to the corner. I cannot remember anything until I walked into the hospital.

That is ten minutes of unaccounted time. I seriously hope I was a good driver. By the time Kevin got to the ER, his temperature spiked up to 104 and they were frantically trying to figure out what was going on inside that boy's body.

We were at the hospital for a few hours during which time Chas and the kids were coming and going. Marissa and Tim had plans to be out of town that weekend. I made it so that they went on their weekend trips. At that time, we had no information and it was best for them to try and keep busy. They hated it and so did I, but I know my children. They despise hospitals and the unknown, and Mansfields are not known for being patient. If they had stayed, we would all have gone crazy and I for one needed to have some control over an already uncontrollable situation. I promised that I would call as soon as we got any news. Kevin was mostly going through CT Scans, strep and flu tests, MRIs, bloodwork, x-rays, and the waiting was painful. We were not much closer to knowing what was going on when they told us that the Critical Care Team was transferring Kevin to the Neuro ICU at Presby Main.

Justin, Chas and I drove together. Oh, Justin… I know he was frightened. He didn't want to talk. How was this going to affect him, the kids? Was this going to change our family? Five minutes into our trip to the ICU, we received a call from a member of the Critical Care Team. My heart was racing again. They wanted us to know that there was traffic approaching and they needed to get Kevin to the ICU as soon as possible so they would be putting on the lights and siren. I thanked God that someone was thinking clearly because if I had seen those sirens and lights go on without warning, I would have needed a bed next to Kevin.

It would be hours before we saw Kevin again. This mama bear was crawling out of her skin. The only thing I was thankful for then was that he was not awake to experience everything that was about to happen. The doctors told us that they were intubating Kevin, inserting a catheter and preforming a spinal tap. We could see him as soon as they examined him and finished all the procedures.

For decades I have lived by the African phrase *It Takes a Village to Raise a Child*. Our village came running the moment we arrived at the hospital. As we sat and paced in the ICU waiting room, in through the door entered our people. They showed up to give support for a member of our village, Kevin Sean Mansfield.

After what seemed like forever, the doctor sat us down for our first of many discussions regarding Kevin. He gave us a possible diagnosis. It could be a flu-like or post infectious encephalitis. He told us that Kevin's chances were 70% survival, 30% death. As I was writing this all down at the time, I inadvertently switched the numbers and froze. *"OH MY GOD,"* I said. I must have lost all color in my face because Chas immediately knew what I thought and told me I had it wrong. It is a comforting feeling to know that your spouse of 25+ years knows you so well. Again, that was another time I thought they might have to put me in the bed next to Kevin. His tests showed positive for the flu and his scans showed swelling with several lesions and bleeds in the thalamus part of the brain. His spinal tap showed lots of blood. Infectious disease doctors and neurologists would be working together to find a diagnosis. They were working on what it wasn't, a process of eliminating, in order to find out what it was.

By midnight, everyone had gone home, except me and Kevin. This would be our first of 42 nights together. I welcomed the peace and quiet and tried to wrap my head around what was happening. Did I say peace and quiet? There were more beeps and alarms then than I could have imagined. I felt like it was in NYC, the hospital that never sleeps. It's 2:00 a.m., and I thought they were throwing a party. All the lights go on in the room, a team of people come in and it's time for an EEG. Twenty-six leads get attached to Kevin's head to check for seizures. After several hours, it was determined that Kevin was not having any seizures. Something good, finally!

Kevin the lady killer, age 13, at his Uncle Michael's wedding.
*(Photograph courtesy of Dawn Mansfield and
published with her permission.)*

KEVIN, MY SON: A FATHER'S PERSPECTIVE

By Charles F. Mansfield III

You can't leave 'cause your heart is there
But, sure, you can't stay 'cause you been somewhere else
You can't cry 'cause you'll look broke down
But you're cryin' anyway 'cause you're all broke down

– Sly & The Family Stone

Chas is Kevin's father, our firstborn son and eldest child. An alumnus of Garden City High School and the Massachusetts Institute of Technology, he also earned an M.B.A. with Academic Distinction from Wake Forest University. A Chartered Financial Analyst (C.F.A.), Chas is the senior director and client portfolio manager of an investment firm based in Washington, D.C. He and his wife Dawn have four children (Tim, 26; Marissa, 22; Kevin, 21; and Justin, 18) and live in Waxhaw, N.C.

These may be the most difficult words I have ever written. I will try to capture the facts here, but understand that I may have some details wrong, because of their gravity and the tragedy they represent to me.

My son, Kevin Sean, was born May 3, 1999, near Charlotte, N.C. He was a happy baby, who loved to twirl his mother's hair as he nursed and was very close with his sister, Marissa, who is nineteen months his senior. As he grew, he developed great athletic ability (probably from trying to "keep up" with his older brother, Tim (six years older) and his sister. In school, he always had a tender, kind and sharing demeanor, was a perennial favorite of his preschool teachers, demonstrated very advanced verbal skills, and had a wonderful, if sarcastic, sense of humor. Over time, Kevin developed a great many fears (some rational, some not), a very finicky palate, a resistance to constructive criticism and a genuine love of the theater.

Kevin was a gifted runner, with very good speed as a youth, but in middle school, he was later than most to reach puberty. As a result, he did not win many sprints, although he would have, if he had stayed with it. Teachers in middle and high school almost universally loved Kevin and his sense of humor, but stated he seemed easily distracted and frequently spoke out of turn. Kevin was diagnosed with Attention Deficit and Hyperactivity Disorder (ADHD), along with Oppositional and Defiance Disorder (ODD). This proved to be a great benefit to Kevin, as the diagnosis allowed him to have extra time on tests, as well as requiring him to be as free of distraction as possible.

Kevin never found school to be enjoyable. Nor did he find an academic pursuit or extracurricular activity that held his interest very long. He longed for greatness, but if he did not experience positive feedback early in his endeavor, he would quit and move on to the next thing. Also, he had very few close friends. It seemed that every time he developed a close friendship, the friend moved away. His best friend from preschool and elementary school was a young man named Nick Shaheen. His family relocated to Indianland, S.C., not too far for adults but too great a distance for young people to maintain a close friendship. Similarly, Robert Bishop was a friend from our neighborhood, who went through elementary school with Kevin but, in middle school, he too moved away; this time the family relocated to the Atlanta, Ga., vicinity. His best friend in middle school was a girl named Annie Grim, the niece of a fraternity brother of mine. They maintained a close friendship throughout middle and high school, and in fact, they maintain a close friendship to this day. Their friendship was completely independent of her uncle's and my friendship, but it was fascinating that these two individuals would form a friendship, nonetheless.

When Kevin entered Charlotte Catholic High School in the fall of 2014, he was popular but had few close friends. His sarcastic and self-deprecating sense of humor was funny, and he had impeccable timing. He also found his calling: theater. He was cast in the fall drama, the first and only freshman ever to be cast in the fall play. He performed very well, alongside his sister, then a junior. He was quite good! He also loved being on stage, although his sister felt a little upstaged. When it was announced that the spring musical would be *Beauty and the Beast*, Marissa auditioned for Belle, while Kevin auditioned for a role in the Ensemble. Both were cast! Marissa was cast as Belle (the lead), and Kevin was cast as LeFou, the comedic sidekick to the male antagonist. In this role, Kevin was able to expand his sense of comedic timing and developed wonderful relationships with young men and women of all grades, freshman through senior. One close relationship of note was Ryan Faucette, who played Gaston, the main antagonist of the musical. Kevin and Ryan became close friends on and off the stage. Peers and teachers all made special mention of his theatrical ability, and Kevin became laser focused on improving his technique in singing, dancing, and acting. He had found his calling!!!

We were understandably thrilled. Kevin performed admirably in every production the school put on through the fall play of his junior year. His most compelling performance was in *Shrek, the Musical* as "Donkey," a talking donkey who is one of the central characters in the show. He dedicated himself from audition preparation through the performances, taking on a professional level of preparation. He was the first main character to memorize his script, and practiced his songs and dance numbers daily, asking Marissa (who did most of the choreography) to help him. His performance was spectacular and memorable!

In December of his junior year, Kevin had a falling out with the main theater teacher over a misunderstanding. Due to Kevin's talent and dedication, Kevin, as a junior had become the de facto face of the Charlotte Catholic theater program, and as Christmastime was approaching, excitement was building because traditionally the spring musical was revealed before the Christmas break. There had been a great deal of discussion and numerous guesses by the theatrical student body regarding what the show might be. Kevin's best guess turned out to be incorrect, but the rumor mill brought another show to his mind. One of his friends had told him what the show was to be. Because of Kevin's notoriety and the fact that he has always been talkative, he was blamed for revealing the musical before the ceremonial reveal. Thus, the teacher was under the impression that Kevin had "leaked" the name of the upcoming spring musical, and sent him this email:

> ***We wanted today to be a surprise for a lot of people. You have ruined that surprise with your excessive chatting. You have a tendency to be overly contemptible and robust in your personality which is turning people away. [A colleague] and I discussed that it might be best if you were not at the meeting today so that other students who have not heard can enjoy the experience of being excited with their peers. We want your theatre experience your junior year to be great, but you are making that difficult, as we have discussed before. Thank you for understanding.***

So, this teacher ostracized Kevin from the only group with which Kevin identified. Needless to say, Kevin was heartbroken and embarrassed, and after meeting with the teachers involved and the school administration, Kevin, Dawn and I decided to pull Kevin out of Charlotte Catholic High School and home school him.

While the home school obviously was not producing a "school musical," Kevin seemed excited. He was planning to audition for local theater groups and continued his studies in the theater arts. He understood the importance of finishing his high school studies, and while there were certainly times when he needed some prodding, he was genuinely eager to uphold his responsibilities. He remained close with some of his friends, most notably Ryan (who also had left Charlotte Catholic over a falling out with the same theater teacher) and Annie (who ended up being home schooled as well).

There was one other tremendous benefit to home schooling: Kevin could take a job during the school year! At first, like many teens, he resisted getting a job. After all, it is much easier to live at home and let your parents do the hard work of supporting you financially. However, he grudgingly got a job at Chick Fil-A and quickly came to appreciate the ability to earn some money of his own. He became a tremendously generous person. He also found that Chick Fil-A did not suit him; he changed to become a student-teacher in the Charlotte-Mecklenburg Schools Afterschool Program. He quickly became a favorite of the students, playing sports with them, and generally enjoying the role. Sadly, it was at this job that he probably contracted his illness.

He was by no means perfect. Like most young people, he would occasionally get into heated arguments with his parents and his siblings. He felt emotions so deeply that anger and fear would sometimes overcome his usually joyful and generous nature, and occasionally, he felt like he could and should boss his siblings around. One thing I should mention: Kevin, more than his siblings, was obsessively passionate about Walt Disney World. The entire family loved Disney but Kevin was unabashed about it. He even had put together a Powerpoint presentation a couple of years earlier, as we planned a vacation to Walt Disney World, laying out options for housing and attractions to maximize our enjoyment of the park. There were eight of us: Dawn, me, Tim, his then-girlfriend, Brooke, Marissa, her boyfriend, Blake, Kevin and our then-16-year-old Justin. This vacation took place in December 2017, and it was very enjoyable! We had hardly returned before Kevin started asking about the *next* Disney vacation!

I spend so much time relating a brief history because what we were all about to endure would make the first 18 ½ years of Kevin's life seem idyllic – not just for Kevin, but for our family as well. He was planning to attend Central Piedmont Community College (CPCC) after he graduated high school. He was planning to continue to hone his craft as a thespian. He was generous, handsome and talented, with the world ahead of him. The reader here should understand that by any measure, Kevin was healthy, happy, loved and loving.

On Monday, February 19, 2018, Kevin went to work at the after-school program, as was his normal Monday routine. He sprained his ankle while playing soccer with the group of young people for whom he was partially responsible. Unable to drive home, Dawn or Marissa picked him up from school and brought him home. He was given a walking boot and crutches and was advised to stay off the ankle for a few days. We did not know it at that time, but he would never work at the school again.

Several days later, on Thursday, February 22, Kevin was running a low-grade fever and complained of nausea. It seemed to us that he probably had contracted the flu and, with four children, we were not overly alarmed. In retrospect, there was one aspect of this episode that was very different from previous ones. Kevin hated going to the doctor. He felt like every time he went, he would get a shot or, worse, a strep test swab of his throat. Oh, how he hated the gagging reflex, and he was VERY sensitive, not even able to swallow the smallest of pills. However, on this night, Kevin said, "Mom, I think I need to go to the doctor." To this day, the recollection of his words causes me to shudder, triggering pangs of guilt.

I was in Greensboro, N.C., on business on the Thursday night and scheduled to return to Charlotte the next day. Tim was my Uber driver. He was trying to earn a little money before he headed off to Paris, France, to continue his baseball career. Since I spent time in Greensboro periodically, I frequently used ride share services. It seemed natural to hire him to drive me. He had driven me up to Greensboro, which is approximately 90 minutes northeast of Charlotte. He was going to spend the night at High Point University, from which he had graduated a year earlier. High Point is only 15 minutes from Greensboro, which allowed him to see his girlfriend, who was still a student at High Point, and his many friends who were also still students.

On Friday, February 23, 2018, at about 1:45 pm, Tim and I were driving back to Charlotte from Greensboro, when this message arrived to my phone via text:

(Image courtesy of Chas Mansfield and published with his permission.)

The XXX-XXX-XXXX was Marissa's cell phone number. I guess my number was the main number on the account, and Verizon was letting me know someone had dialed 911. I was slightly concerned, as Marissa's dorm at UNC Charlotte had had some thefts in the recent weeks. So, I remarked to Tim, "Oh, Marissa just dialed 911. I hope she is ok." With that, I called Marissa's cell phone. My call immediately went to voice mail, implying that she was on the phone at the time. Naturally, I called Dawn's cell. After several rings, my call went to *her* voice mail. Now, fear was rising, but I still figured the emergency was related to Marissa's well-being. With that, Tim's phone rang. It was Marissa. She was hysterical, mumbling through tears that Kevin was unresponsive, and Mom is on the phone with the EMTs, and an ambulance was coming for him and she had to go…

Tim hung up and relayed this conversation to me with confusion and consternation in his eyes. How this 24-year-old man managed to stay on the road is miraculous by itself, and now, I could not make sense out of it. Kevin unresponsive? No way. It was a routine flu. Shortly, Dawn called me. Here is what I recall her saying:

I came home to take Kevin to his doctor appointment and called up the stairs that he needed to get up so we could be on time. After a short while, not hearing any activity, I went upstairs to his room and knocked softly. There was no response, so I opened the door to find him still sleeping. I went in, getting annoyed, and shook him gently. There was no response. I shook him hard, starting to yell…Still, nothing! So, I slapped him! No response. I told Marissa to bring me her phone and sent her to look for Tim. [I think she had forgotten that Tim was with me.] *Marissa was in a panic and couldn't find him, so I called 911. I don't know more than that but the EMTs are here, and I gotta go. I will call when I know more.*

At that moment, I still could not fathom what had happened. It was clear something was very wrong, but I thought maybe his fever had spiked, and that intravenous fluids and Tylenol® would bring him back to consciousness. Tim and I were about an hour from home.

Dawn called my phone again a little while later. She was following the ambulance to Novant Presbyterian Hospital in Matthews, N.C., and told us to meet her there. OK, Kevin would be ok. He was young, healthy (other than the flu), and in professional hands. I immediately called my employer to inform them of the situation and that I was not sure when I would be available. I told them what little I knew, and they had my cell phone number, should they need to reach me.

Tim and I went to the hospital, arriving around 2:45 p.m. Marissa was with Mary Anne Jackson (Blake's mother) in the waiting room. They looked somber and told us where Kevin was. We walked in to see Dawn sitting at Kevin's bedside, holding his hands and talking to him. Kevin's eyes were half-closed, but it seemed like he could hear what was being said. Doctors and nurses were running all sorts of tests but could not isolate what was wrong. It seemed to me that Kevin could respond to simple questions with hand squeezes, but he couldn't open his eyes fully. I took hope from this and when he was taken in for another test, I called my best friend, Leland Maddox, who was Tim's and Justin's longtime baseball coach and who had coached Kevin when he played baseball. He stopped at the hospital to visit, but he was heading to Atlanta, Ga., for a tournament with one of the younger Team Carolina (TC) baseball teams.

After I saw Leland, Dawn and I agreed I should go get Justin, since it was becoming apparent that this would not be a simple, short-term stay. Justin was with the school baseball team, playing in a scrimmage, blissfully unaware of the day's occurrences. I arrived at the field and waited for the inning to end. Then, I called the coach over and told him, "Justin's brother is in the hospital, unresponsive. If you do not need Justin, may I take him out of the scrimmage?" The coach assented, and I met Justin outside the fence. He was clearly nervous, expecting bad news, but the news I delivered was so unexpected that it jarred him visibly. I asked if he was capable of driving home, and I would follow him and take him to the hospital. He said yes, but he said he didn't want to go to the hospital.

Justin has always been uncomfortable in hospitals, probably because of the unusually high number of Emergency Room visits he has endured. I followed him home, where he changed his clothes, and we began to speak.

"Dad, I really don't want to go to the hospital."

"Justin, you need to go." Dawn and I had anticipated his hesitation and reticence. "Remember when Grandma died, how you did not want to be in her room, and when she died you regretted not having said goodbye?" At this, his eyes moistened.

"I'm not ready to say goodbye!!!"

"None of us are, son. Which is exactly why we all need to be there, so he knows we love him and support him. I don't know what he can hear or feel, but if he can sense us at all, we need to be there!"

We drove over to the hospital, where by now Lisa Maddox (Leland's wife) and some other close friends had arrived to support us. Additionally, the hospital had identified swelling in his brain, and while the cause of the swelling was still unknown, they prepared Kevin for transport by ambulance to the Neurological Intensive Care Unit, about 10 miles away in downtown Charlotte. We followed.

We waited in the Neuro-ICU waiting room for hours. A steady stream of friends was there. Lisa Maddox never wavered. She was always present and supportive. Leland never was away from my phone calls. He would take my call anywhere, anytime. JJ Davis and Trey Tinch (two of the TC coaches) were frequently present and waited until late in the night. Xander Maddox (Leland's son and one of Tim's best friends) and his then-girlfriend were also there. Pam Chila and Shirley Orton (Dawn's soul sisters) were absolute rocks for Dawn. They both were there that night and, at different times, they would take the other kids out of the waiting room to go and talk. The gratitude I feel for these people can never be expressed for the simple reason that any expression would be inadequate. We could not possibly have made it through this without our village. I even got a call from Justin's school baseball coach, following up and asking if everything was ok.

At approximately 10 p.m. (it could have been 2 a.m....this detail is fuzzy), the neurologist on duty came into the waiting room to give us an update on Kevin's condition. Dawn asked Pam to join us for her support, and so that Pam could ask questions, as her son Nick had died of brain cancer, and she was accustomed to asking hard questions of a neurologist. She was amazing. We could not ask for better friends! The doctor told us that all the tests indicate that the brain was swelling, and that he was indeed quite sick, but they had been able to rule out many of the most life-threatening illnesses. Kevin's initial brain activity showed positive signs, but the doctor did say that the part of the brain that was swelling was the part that we usually associate with "wakefulness." I asked what that meant, and he replied by saying the eyelids may droop, he may be slower to respond, he may just seem tired more frequently, but he emphasized this: "It would be a mistake at this point to expect that Kevin would be unchanged when or if he wakes up." In other words, Dawn and I were being prepared for what is a parent's worst nightmare. At this point, I knew our lives were changing.

As the family grapevine and social media did their things, the phone rang periodically with friends and family calling with messages of love and support, horror and sadness, but also of hope. One such call came from my first cousin, Jeff Petrillo. We are the two oldest of our generation of "Locasto girl offspring." I was born in April of 1968, and he was born in August of that year. The Petrillos and the Mansfields were and are as close as any sets of first cousins have been, and Jeff was even one of my groomsmen. Jeff has had a great career in nursing, most of which was earned in a variety of high-stress environments, such as Emergency Rooms, MedEvac, etc. Currently, Jeff practices as a Nurse Anesthetist, so when he called, I was eager to hear what his experiences were with such situations. We still had no idea at this point what was causing the issues, but we were slowly ruling out different possibilities. So, when Jeff asked what was happening and what the doctors were saying, he understood the gravity. He told me:

> *"The doctors are telling you the worst-case scenario so that you don't build false hope. The most important thing for you and Dawn to do is to focus on the next step of recovery. DO NOT think through all the possible outcomes or the odds of any particular outcome. Let the doctors and nurses figure all that out. Your focus cannot be on the cause of this; just focus on the next stage of recovery. Right now, that is when he wakes up. ALL your energy should be focused on how to support him when that happens! Then it will be walking, then eating, then talking etc."*

This was probably the best advice I could have been given because it allowed me to be practical and supportive to my son, my wife and our other children. I tend to overanalyze situations but overanalyzing this one might have killed me. I will forever be grateful to Jeff for giving me the tools to maintain sanity.

When it became clear that Kevin would not be awakening that Friday night, Dawn and I realized that we had not eaten, Justin had not eaten (Pam, Shirley and the Maddoxes had fed him a little but we were just a little preoccupied!), and we had two dogs at home that would not handle being left alone overnight. So, Dawn and I put together a plan. We were adamant that Kevin not be left alone. WHEN he awoke, we wanted one of us to be right there beside him. He has never been comfortable around doctor's offices, needles and medical devices, and we could only imagine his fear if he woke up alone. It was decided that Dawn would stay with him, and I would man the homefront.

I went home to get Dawn some pajamas and toiletries, as well as a change of clothes for Kevin. I walked the dogs, got some food for Justin and returned to the hospital. By the time I returned, they had set Kevin up in a room. My heart stopped when I saw him! He was unconscious, elevated about ¾, mouth agape, intubated, attached to a respirator, with a feeding tube up his nose. Wires were everywhere, monitoring his cardiac and pulmonary activity. Of course, there were the sounds of an intensive care unit, beeping and hissing, and virtually constant activity, as nurses and doctors made frequent rounds. Even with all that noise, it was ghostly quiet. As I looked at my 18-year-old son, it occurred to me that he should be out with friends on a Friday night, or watching a college basketball game or something life-affirming. Whatever it should have been, it should NOT have been lying in an ICU, requiring mechanical assistance to breathe!

Dawn and I went down to the cafeteria, leaving Lisa Maddox and Shirley Orton (I think!) with Kevin. We were alone for the first time since she had discovered our son, lying in his urine-soaked bed, unable to communicate or respond meaningfully to the sound of her voice. I know she felt guilty, but I felt like an utter failure. Parents are supposed to protect their children. An 18-year-old should not need breathing assistance from THE FLU! I know the reader will think, "There is nothing you could have done." That is the rational approach. In my mind, I certainly knew that, but we were running purely on emotion. When we went back to Kevin's room, there had not been any change. I then made one desperate plea that I thought might inspire him to awaken. Recall that Kevin was and is our Disney fanatic. I said, "Kevin, if you open your eyes and walk out of here right now, we will go to Disney World for two weeks tomorrow!" If that did not elicit a response, nothing would! Dawn and I decided I would go home, and try to sleep for a little while, and she would stay with him. The hospital staff was AMAZING!!! They offered her drinks, food, blankets, pillows…

really, anything that might make a devastated mother just a bit more comfortable. We said good night, and I proceeded home.

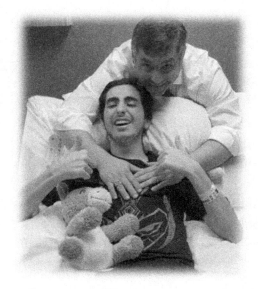

Chas and post-coma Kevin giving two thumbs up.
Note that Donkey has four hooves up.
*(Photograph courtesy of Dawn Mansfield and
published with her permission.)*

The next morning, I awoke, tended to the dogs' needs, and asked if Justin wanted to come with me to the hospital. Tim and Marissa had long-standing plans to be out of town, so they were not there. At that time, with so few answers, we made sure they kept things as normal as possible. Understandably, Justin at 16 did not want to be at the hospital all day. He made plans with friends for the entire day, while he planned to come to the hospital that evening, but it was imperative that I be present at the hospital to support my wife and son. Dawn needed to get out of that hospital for a little while, and I knew she would not leave his bedside unless I were taking her place.

Kevin was still unconscious, and the activity in the room was virtually constant, with nurses keeping his sheets, gown and body clean, checking his vitals every hour or two. Additionally, doctors were still running tests. There were two primary doctors, one an infectious disease specialist who confirmed the flu diagnosis but also identified another viral infection. The other, of course, was the neurologist. There were three different neurologists who were assigned to the ICU. Saturday, February 24th, was a tough day because there was not a lot of new information. However, what did occur was proof positive of the existence of God.

At that point, we had lived in Charlotte approximately 22 years, almost 19 of which were at the same address. We had volunteered at our local recreation association and at church, and were well-known in our neighborhood, since our home was central and clearly visible from the most used road in the area. Our kids were often playing football or wiffleball in the front yard, so we knew most of our neighbors, and they knew us. The miracle came as our various communities came together to create a meal schedule, bake cakes, cookies, pies and muffins, tend to our yard, etc. There was not a single chore untended. Our only focus was Kevin's recovery. The mother of one of Justin's classmates even made sure that Justin had lunch every day, sending along an extra lunch with her son to make sure that Justin did not go hungry. Every hour we had volunteered, every relationship we had invested in…they all paid dividends that weekend and in the coming weeks.

Sunday through Wednesday was an endless stream of tests and doctors, and trying to care for our household. On Monday, I had a job interview in Washington, D.C. I had contemplated cancelling until this situation had been resolved, but Dawn reminded me that Kevin was unlikely to awaken on Monday, as his fever had not yet subsided, and we barely had a diagnosis yet. The hiring manager knew the situation, and when I walked into his office, I apologized in advance, but I was going to leave my phone on, and, if it rang, I would need to take it. He was understanding and accommodating, as were all five of the people with whom I met that day. I felt a bit like the walking dead, and I told the recruiter I was not sure what kind of impression I had made. Apparently, I made enough of a good impression. The firm ended up offering me a job!

Tuesday, we had a really hard day. Dr. McWilliams met with Dawn and me privately, while Shirley stayed with Kevin. The doctor asked us to consider which of two treatments we wanted to pursue: Intravenous Immuno Globulin (IVIG) or Plasmapheresis. IVIG was easier to administer but carried a risk of clotting, potentially causing a stroke. Plasmapheresis carried fewer risks but was administered over time. It was not easy to administer. The process entailed filtering the disease out of his bloodstream by replacing his blood plasma with albumin. The filtering would occur over a five- to seven-day course.

Visitors streamed in. A neighbor brought a prayer group of women to pray over Kevin. A priest came to pray for Kevin and administer the Anointing of the Sick (to be certain, this was unsettling).

On Wednesday, Kevin's fever stayed between 99 and 100 degrees but we had some promising signs. His urine output was good, and he was able to wiggle his toe when asked, despite still being unable to open his eyes or respond verbally.

Dawn and I had settled into a routine. I would rise early, walk the dogs and take out of the freezer one of the many meals our neighbors had made. I would then proceed to the hospital, usually by roughly 7:30, so that Dawn could go to her work teaching four-year-olds. When school let out, she would go home, shower, change her clothes, and return to the hospital, usually with dinner or some heavy snacks.

That evening brought a shock to Dawn and me. Dr. McWilliams sat down with us again and told us she thought they had discovered his diagnosis, a condition called Acute Necrotizing Encephalopathy Myelitis (ANEM). From what they could tell, neither the flu nor the unnamed virus was particularly strong, but the combination had overwhelmed Kevin's immune system, which turned to eat the lining of the nerves in his brain. The myelin sheath insulates the nerves, much like the plastic coating insulates copper wire. That insulation allows the nervous impulses from the brain to the rest of the body to flow efficiently and quickly.

Dr. McWilliams continued that there are only about 20,000 cases of this worldwide, and mostly in the developing world. It was almost never observed in the United States. To make Kevin's case even more rare, when it did occur, it was almost always as an outgrowth of Flu type A. Kevin's case entailed type B, the type that was NOT incorporated into the vaccine. Kevin was only the SECOND known case of this occurring! (He did not receive a flu vaccine, but it would not have mattered!) Fortunately for us, Dr. McWilliams' medical mentor had treated the first such case in the Cleveland, Oh., area, so Dr. McWilliams had spoken with him and they agreed that this was what was affecting Kevin.

Dr. McWilliams told us that Kevin had a 30% chance of dying! Poor Dawn! I saw her face go white as she thought the doctor had said a 30% chance of *living*! After clarifying for Dawn, the doctor continued. He has lesions in his skull, and they were not sure when he would wake up. Additionally, she told us how grave Kevin's situation was. He had a new baseline. In other words, our expectations were being adjusted downward again. She stated that our son was expected to have severe disabilities, if he awoke. These disabilities would affect his cognition, thinking, personality and memory, and he might struggle to walk again. He might be bound to a wheelchair!

This was obviously disheartening news! As I have mentioned, Dawn was surrounded by her people, Pam and Shirley. She kept asking me who I wanted to see. In retrospect, my response seems ludicrous and stupid, but I think I was just so focused on Kevin that he was the only person I wanted to see. Nonetheless, as I sat with Kevin that night, trying to occupy myself with work, a person walked into the room who was so unexpected, it initially did not make any sense to my stressed, exhausted brain. My cousin, Greg Petrillo (Jeff's brother), who lives in the Philadelphia, Pa., vicinity, had business nearby and visited unannounced. The juxtaposition of Greg standing in the doorway in Charlotte, N.C., was overwhelming; I started to say, "What the h&## are you doing here?" but before I could finish, my face screwed itself up into a mask of pain and grief, and tears flowed freely, with heaving sobs, as my cousin and I just hugged and held each other. Greg was once a volunteer EMT, and he kept asking questions that indicated that the myriad drugs and tests all made sense to him, though Dawn and I still felt clueless. I don't know if I even said "Thank you" to Greg, but hope he knows how much that visit meant to me. I am frequently asked how I know that God exists. Well, this visit and its timing are one of many "proof points."

Obviously, our conversation with Dr. McWilliams was disheartening, but we continued to have faith. We were receiving daily messages from people we had not seen in decades. A friend launched a GoFundMe to raise money to help with what would be massive hospital bills. We received Mass cards and prayer intentions from around the world, including the Vatican. Our village, as Dawn refers to them, included people who had never met Kevin – some had never met Dawn or me – but their fondness for my parents or aunts or uncles or cousins or friends was enough to inspire them to pray for my son! Prayer WORKS!

That night, we needed a positive sign. According to Dawn, that night Kevin opened his eyes slightly and started to cry some. Thank you! The next day saw Kevin's first round of plasmapheresis. On Friday, March 2nd, seven days after Dawn had found him, Kevin opened his eyes. Dawn and I were both in the room. I was looking directly at him when they opened, and I said, as calmly and clearly as I could, "Dawn, his eyes are open, and they are staying open!" Dawn got a nurse, who immediately ran in to begin talking to Kevin so he could gather his wits and bearings. He was responding to commands but was still intubated and connected to lots of monitoring equipment, so we did not want him to pull any tubes or wires. He then went back to sleep.

What a wonderful feeling it was to see those eyes! The next few days were a blur! Still, I couldn't help feeling overwhelmingly positive. He could not speak. He was still intubated. He could not eat. He was awake, though!!! He was definitely unsettled – well, who wouldn't be?! He would get particularly restless periodically, and we couldn't figure out what he was trying to say or do – how frustrating! Finally, we realized he needed to relieve himself, but had forgotten that he had a catheter. We would remind him, he would settle, and the urine bag hooked on his bed would fill. There were some heartbreaking moments, like when he was only capable of seeing double because one of his optical nerves was damaged. There were also huge triumphs, even though most people would view these as baby steps. For example, when he would accomplish a movement that his physical therapists were suggesting, such as a high five or sticking out his tongue or kicking his feet, he would look at Dawn or me with a smile and say, "I did it!" I have never been prouder!

There were also some wonderful moments that our entire family experienced. One was a social media post which showed six hands touching Kevin's, with his hand being central to the photo. The other five were ours, and we attached the so-called hashtag, "#AllHandsIn4Kevin." This became a source of inspiration to us. We also designed and sold t-shirts as a fundraising effort. The front had this message on the left breast: $\frac{FAITH}{FEAR}$, with the T of FAITH in the shape of a cross, indicating our Catholic faith. On the back of the shirt is written, "Baby Steps Can Be Taken at Any Age." This has also inspired others, a fact of which we are very proud.

That young man had to learn how to swallow, speak, stand up, walk, take stairs, brush his teeth, eat, feed himself, remember things (his memory was affected by this event). He never once lost his sense of humor. After the week he spent in his coma, he spent another week in ICU. Then, there was a week in what the hospital called a "step-down" unit. We would call it a "leap-down." The frequency of care was inadequate for what this man had gone through. He could not communicate, and he was connected to feeding and monitoring machines but, when he called, the nurses responded with all the urgency of grass growing. Still, he continued to make tremendous progress. His first steps were taken during this period. His physical therapists got him up on the walker and talked him through each step. He only got five or six steps before he was exhausted but he was supporting 75-80% of his weight on his legs and the walker. I remember seeing the fear in his eyes and the confusion that his legs no longer worked. Still, he kept going, not quitting ever! Fortunately, after a week, he was transferred to an in-patient rehabilitation center.

While we were certainly glad to be leaving the hospital, I looked back on the wonderful caregivers he had. They were not only attentive to his needs but always respectful and treated him with humanity and love, even while he was in his coma. Additionally, they were caring for Dawn and made sure her needs were met. In case you are unaware, Dawn had yet to spend a single night away from Kevin. That Mama Bear was FIERCE.

At the rehab center, as Kevin's care moved from medical life-saving to a phase of life-supporting, our family started to be prepared for Kevin's return home…Oh my God! We allowed ourselves to think of him returning home! Three weeks earlier, I was praying to see my son's eyes again. As I write this, tears of joy and gratitude are returning to my eyes, as they were then. The day he was transferred, I was out of town on business but, upon my return, I walked into Kevin's room, and Tim, Brooke, Marissa, Blake, Dawn and Justin were all around him. He looked over, and I delivered what I thought was going to be a supportive, inspirational, serious message:

"Kevin, God has given you a tremendous opportunity. I know it is hard to see the good that can come from this, but I believe that God has a strong message that he wants you to deliver."

"Yeah," Kevin interrupted with a smile. "Don't fart with your pants down!"

After a momentary pause, the entire room erupted into hysterical laughter. Heeee's Baaack!! The laughter was a response in part to the line itself, and the timing of the line was perfect! However, more than a little bit of the laughter came from an overwhelming relief that Kevin's personality and sense of humor were intact!

We had visitors throughout the next few weeks. Kevin was given a very rigorous daily regimen of therapy. One day, we arranged for a very special visitor. Jeter, Kevin's dog and loyal companion, a Maltese-Yorkshire terrier crossbreed, was allowed to spend the day with Kevin in the outdoor courtyard. Kevin sat in his wheelchair and Jeter sat next to him while we talked. Kevin could not speak clearly but he seemed genuinely happy to see Jeter, and Jeter seemed content to sit next to him and spend the day there.

Finally, on Thursday, April 5th, Kevin was released from the rehab center. He had lost thirty pounds, still had a feeding tube in his abdomen, could not yet stand or walk for even moderate periods of time, and he had glasses with a frosted lens covering his left eye because he had double vision. He still needed help to dress himself completely. We hired nurses to come care for Kevin in the mornings when Dawn and I had to go to work. Dawn would be home in the afternoon, when she would relieve the nurse and she would shuttle Kevin to his myriad doctor appointments. Of Kevin's forty-two nights away from home, Dawn had spent forty-one of them by his side. The lone outlier saw me replace my dedicated, relentless, strong wife.

Our trials were not yet complete. On Friday, April 13th, my employer let me go. I was terminated, effective immediately. We were flabbergasted. My employer intimated that Kevin's ordeal had revealed that they needed their Chief Investment Officer to be present in Greensboro, N.C., and they needed him to be able to travel liberally. They also said something I never thought I would hear, "You are too smart for a small company like ours." I was stunned, to be certain. The most interesting thing they said though, was "If you launch a business, don't rule us out as a client or reference." They offered me a separation package as compensation. I did consult a Family Medical Leave Act attorney who advised me to take the package. Without hard evidence, we could file suit and begin discovery, with no guarantee, or take the compensation and move on. That seemed a wiser approach.

I remained unemployed but very active, through May. On June 6, 2018, I started a job with ICMA-RC as a Senior Director, Client Portfolio Manager, headquartered in Washington, D.C. The location was and remains less than ideal but it is a great firm for which to work. My boss and senior management never lose sight of employees' humanity, and the HR policies are tremendously supportive of work-life balance. The benefit package is generous, and my compensation is fair. I could not ask for a better situation. I remain grateful for all we have been through, though I would not be eager to repeat it!

Kevin earned his high school diploma in December 2018. With every other challenge he had to endure, we as his parents were incredibly proud. Today, Kevin walks comfortably. He does not run well, but he no longer fears running. In fact, his brothers, he and I play touch football every Thanksgiving. While he is not the athletic threat he once was, he participates and competes. He still has tremors but his vision is almost back to 100%. He only experiences double vision when he looks far to the left. He is unable to work currently but he continues therapies and rehabilitation, and he hopes to live independently one day.

The prayers, the love, the village… It all had worked! In fact, it brought together my family and my marriage in ways that nothing else had ever done. It was as if this event caused us all to latch on to each other and hold on for dear life. We know only too well the value of human life, and none of us takes time together for granted.

From the bottom of my heart, I sincerely thank each of you who thought of us. I offer a blank check – not necessarily financial – if I can do anything to help, I remain in your debt. I stand by my comments to Kevin; that God has given us a strong message through this ordeal. "If He brings you to it, He will bring you through it!" I do not believe God promises us an easy life, but His grace can bring good from a bad situation. This I have seen firsthand. We have the gift of each other, and I will never forget God's gift to us: Kevin, yes, but more than that, the many people who kept faith and love when we were consumed by fear and doubt.

Thank you! Thank you! Thank you!

WE NEEDED TO KNOW THAT EVERYTHING WOULD BE OKAY

By Timothy Charles Mansfield

*It's strong and it's sudden, and it's cruel sometimes /
But it might just save your life / That's the power of love.*

– Huey Lewis and the News

Tim, 26, is our eldest grandchild. On May 6, 2017, he graduated with honors from High Point University (High Point, North Carolina) where he played varsity baseball for the Panthers. Following a three-game sweep of the Charleston Southern University Buccaneers, with whom his team had up to then been tied in the Big South Conference standings, he was named the Big South Player of the Week, having batted .727 during the weekend series. Tim went eight for eleven in the three games against the Buccaneers and accounted for nine of the Panthers' 13 runs in the series with five RBIs and four runs scored. A redshirt-senior, he recorded multiple hits in every game and finished the weekend with three doubles and three stolen bases. My wife Mame and I attended all three games and were thrilled to witness Tim's extraordinary performance.

In an interview following his team's impressive sweep, Panthers' head coach Craig Cozart described Tim as "a tremendous competitor at the plate" and a player who "embodies what we want out of our offense." He then cited Tim's "tenacity" and "competitiveness." Tim has since received Big South All Conference honors. A significant factor in this recognition, Tim's fifteen strikeouts tied him for first place in the Big South for the fewest number of strikeouts for players with at least 150 plate appearances. In other words, he struck out only nine percent of the time.

In 2018 Tim played professional baseball for the Lions of Savigny-sur-Orge outside Paris, France. He was also named to the French baseball league's all-star team, and knocked in his team's tying run in the all-star game, after which his team went on to victory.

Formerly director of player development at Koa Sports, Tim later served at Baseball Info Solutions as a baseball scout and is currently a physical trainer.

Tim is the author of "More Than a Game—God is Forever," which was published in Chuck's fourth book, LEADERSHIP: In Action, Thought and Word *and "It's Not 'Don't Strike Out' But 'Hit This Pitch'" in his grandfather's second book,* BITS AND PIECES: Stories to Soothe the Soul or Raise the Hackles.

February of '18 was an exciting time. I was seven months removed from major hip surgery and cleared to train at full speed in preparation for my first professional season in the French Baseball Top Division. While I spent most of my time in the gym or the batting cages, I made my money by driving for Uber. Multiple times a week I would drive my Dad from Charlotte to his job in Greensboro. While he was at the office, I would train at my alma mater—High Point University—before hanging with my old friends still in school. Everything seemed to be perfect. Until it wasn't.

On this particular day, a Friday, February 23rd, my Dad and I were getting ready to return to Charlotte. We stopped for lunch and when we got in the car, he received a notification on his phone that my sister, Marissa, had called 9-1-1. Very confused as to why, we frantically tried to get in touch with anybody back home. After a few tries, I was finally able to get hold of a hysterical Marissa. She informed us that my brother, Kevin, who had been dealing with a severe case of the flu for a few days, was found unresponsive and needed to be rushed to the hospital. For the next one and a half hours my mind raced. I had never been so scared. When we got to the emergency room, we saw that Kevin was dealing with swelling in the brain and mostly unresponsive, aside from the occasional hand squeeze when you asked him a question. After a few hours in the ER, Kevin was rushed to the ICU. We weren't aware of the battle that lay ahead.

Kevin was in a coma for a week. As he was completely unresponsive, we weren't sure if or when he would come back to us. Seeing him in the condition he was in was the single hardest time of my life, and without the friends and family who spent countless hours by our side and sending us prayers from afar, I'm not sure I would've been as composed as I was. Yet, over the following month, Kevin made progress day by day and, before we knew it, he was back home where he belongs.

To this day, Kevin remains the same funny and charismatic guy he's always been. I thank the good Lord every single day for keeping my brother around. While we struggled to understand why, we knew God was putting Kevin in this situation for a reason and it forced us to pull ourselves closer to Him. Over time the negative images that haunted me every day while Kevin was in ICU—the cords, the wires, the silence, the beeping—have begun to fade and I seem to only remember the never ending prayers, the many, many welcome visitors (both anticipated and surprise), and all the other uplifting moments that brought my family closer than we've ever been. I'm still not sure what the reason God had for putting my baby brother through this turmoil, but I realize now just how much I took my relationships with him, my other two siblings and my parents for granted.

These last two years have taught me so much about what it truly means to be a FAMILY. The day we moved Kevin from the step-down unit at the hospital to inpatient rehab, my Dad, my other brother, Justin, and I were sitting with him in his room. Dad looked at Kev with tears in his eyes and asked, "Kev, I know it's hard to see, but God is using you to send the world an important message. Do you know what that is?"

"Don't fart with your pants down." In that moment, we all could breathe again. That six-word phrase was all we needed to know that everything would be okay. He was the same kid. And truthfully, that's what I've learned from all of this—that even in the darkest times, God and the ones you love most will get you through anything; that faith can be tested day in and day out but, when firm, can never be defeated; and yes, no matter what, NEVER fart with your pants down.

Tim hugging and saying goodbye to Kevin as Tim was leaving for six months to play professional baseball in France in 2018. Kevin would not let go.
(Photograph courtesy of Dawn Mansfield and published with her permission.)

LITTLE BROTHERS ARE WORTH EVERYTHING

By Marissa Hope Mansfield

Marissa, 22, is Kevin's elder sister and now a senior at the University of North Carolina-Charlotte. The two are best friends. She posted this article on Facebook on March 27, 2018, and described herself as "Just a college kid, telling her story piece by piece. Welcome to a look into my world."

Well done, Princess.

Marissa, Donkey and Kevin.
(Photograph courtesy of Dawn Mansfield and published with her permission.)

These past few weeks turned my world upside down. On February 23, my younger brother was found unconscious and unresponsive. We called 911 and waited for EMS to take him to the emergency room. We only hoped it was dehydration from throwing up, but they still had no official diagnosis.

They ran multiple tests to rule certain diseases out. The infectious disease team worked with him to come up with an accurate prognosis. After a few spinal taps, MRIs and CT scans, they came to the conclusion that he had encephalitis (swelling of the brain). Later that night, they transferred him from the ER to the Neuro ICU at the main hospital uptown. He lay here, lifeless, in a coma for an entire week. My he art shattered and physically hurt watching my brother not being himself. Sitting there, looking at my little brother with a breathing tube down his throat, a feeding tube down his nose, not moving and face so swollen, physically hurt me. I told myself that I needed to be strong for him and be there for him, but it was exhausting. It took every ounce of energy from my body. I was there every second that I could be. I took off school for a week (plus a week for spring break) and also slept there! He was no longer my brother that I fight with, he was my baby that I needed to care for.

Within the time span of his coma we witnessed little victories, until we had our dreaded "diagnosis meeting" with the doctor. She sat us down and told us "It's complicated." I knew immediately that what needed to be said wasn't going to be good news. The doctor told us that his thalamus was damaged. That meant his consciousness was going to be an issue. The thalamus is in charge of consciousness and motor skills. We discovered that Kevin had what they call Acute Necrotizing Encephalopathy Myelitis (ANEM). He is only the second case **EVER** to stem from flu B (the more intense strain)! Don't bother looking it up, because there's no information on it! Short explanation: His brain was so swollen that the immune system started attacking itself. They said that it's going to be a long and exhausting process and that we just have to take it step by step and not look too far ahead. She told us that Kevin might not be the same Kevin he once was. They said he may be a completely different person.

Kevin was in a coma for about a week before they extubated him (took his breathing tube out). Once extubated, he began to wake up and try to communicate with us. He would squeeze our hands and open his eyes. I never knew looking into someone's eyes would be so enjoyable and relieving. I found myself saying "Just open your eyes" and "Oh, what I'd give to see those eyes again." He would try communicating with us through speech, but his vocal chords had been so affected from the tube that it made talking extremely difficult. We gave him a whiteboard to try and write. That made it slightly easier, but still not like it was before.

Two weeks later, almost to the second, we were discharged from ICU and placed in a step-down unit. It was less intense care, and a much less friendly place. We had gotten to know the ICU nurses and formed very close relationships with them. The step-down nurses only arrived if they were called. It was a very stressful few days.

About a week later, he was transferred from the step-down unit at Presbyterian to Carolina Rehabilitation at CMC. He gets his own room and bathroom. He has therapy all day from 8 a.m. to about 4 p.m., depending on the day. He has physical therapy, occupational therapy and speech therapy. He loves his nurses and therapists. Every day, he has a new story to tell them about what he did the day before, even if it's the same person.

He's really looking forward to coming home and getting to see his dog, Jeter. We brought Jeter to the rehab center once for a visit and it's the happiest I've seen Kevin during this entire journey.

Kevin and Jeter reunited.
(Photograph courtesy of Dawn Mansfield and published with her permission.)

He truly is our miracle. We don't know where we'd be today without the help from friends and family, but also without the love, support, and the overwhelming amount of prayers that have been sent our way.

If we keep at the pace we're at, Kevin will be discharged and allowed to go home on April 5!!! T-10 days from today! I can't wait to see my little brother back in action. It's time to start our new lives as a family and our new normal routine.

I've always had a close relationship with my brother but I believe this truly brought us even closer. Kevin is not only my brother, but my best friend, fighter BUT most importantly my HERO. I love you so so much, Bub, and I'm so proud of the work you've put in thus far.

This journey is nowhere near over, but baby steps can be taken at any age.

JUST IN TIME

By Justin Conner Mansfield

Justin, 18, is our third grandson and youngest grandchild. A senior at Charlotte Catholic High School, he is an excellent baseball player and a fine young man.

The heart-wrenching emotions he felt and describes below about his elder brother Kevin and his illness are palpable.

Thank you, Justin.

Coach said, "Justin, pack up and meet your Dad outside the dugout."

My first thought was that someone had died. Dad told me what happened. He said, "Kevin is unconscious and at the hospital right now. Are you able to drive your car home?"

As I drove home, I was holding back tears.

"Why is this happening? How is this happening?" At home, I got in Dad's car but didn't want to go to the hospital.

Dad said, "Remember when you didn't see grandma before she died and you have felt guilty since. You need to see Kevin."

"I'm not ready to say goodbye."

Dad said, "None of us are."

When we got to the hospital, we saw Mr. Maddox, who stopped by on his way to Atlanta. Tim was inside waiting for me and he took me back to see Kevin. That was right before they transported him to the Neuro ICU at the main hospital uptown. I was scared. Marissa and Tim were going out of town before Kevin got sick and Mom made them go. Until we knew what was going on, it was best to keep them busy. I don't like hospitals in general, and didn't want to be there, especially without Marissa and Tim. I felt alone.

Dad and I drove uptown and I used a dozen tissues even though I was trying to hold back from crying. We waited in the waiting room for what seemed liked forever, and lots of people started coming in to stay with us. Mom told Aunt Pamie and Shirley (Mom's soul sisters) to take me away from there for a bit so we went to Bojangles. When I returned, the doctor on duty took us into a conference room to discuss Kevin. All I heard him say was "critical;" I totally missed the part about him being "stable." I left the room and cried.

Aunt Pamie came out of the room with me and we sat on the floor. She told me, "Nick [her late son, a cancer victim who passed away in his early teens] would never let anything happen to Kevin." It was comforting but I was drained and just wanted to get out of there.

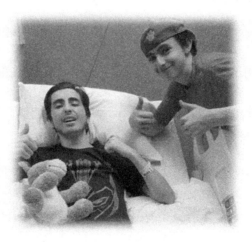

Kevin and Justin both giving two thumbs up.
Again Donkey has four hooves up.
(Photograph courtesy of Dawn Mansfield and published with her permission.)

MAMIE'S MEMORIES

By Mary Ann Mansfield

But now faith, hope, and love remain – these three. The greatest of these is love.

– 1 Corinthians 13:13

The phone rang late Friday afternoon. When I heard Dawn's voice, I was surprised and totally unprepared for her message. Kevin lay comatose in the hospital undergoing a series of tests to determine a diagnosis. He had been suffering from the flu for a few days but finding him unconscious and unresponsive after returning home from work was shocking. She asked us to pray.

We used to joke that the "Stewart hotline" was more effective than social media in getting news out to the family. (Kevin's paternal great-grandmother was one of five girls née Stewart.) We called everyone we knew, contacted our huge network of friends and family, and enlisted a prayer chain of thousands around the world. Didn't tragedy like this happen to *other* people?

Kevin in the arms of his paternal great-grandmother, Bernice Locasto, in Westhampton, N.Y., summer 1999. *(Photograph courtesy of Mary Ann Mansfield and published with her permission.)*

For the next few days, I kept remembering the 18-year-old's life from a grandmother's perspective. Kevin was an adorable, smart baby, vividly pictured in my mind sleeping on my visiting mother's shoulder and twirling his mother's hair every time he nursed. Nineteen months younger than his sister Marissa, he was an infinitely easier-going baby than she! As he grew, Marissa became his good friend, although my take on their adventures together sometimes made that questionable. I particularly remember her instructing Kevin to write with a crayon on the wall with her, and then reported *his* misdeed instantly to their parents. Unfortunately for both children, Momma was very smart and identified the *two different* handwritings.

Kevin was the "middle child" although not technically. Tim is six years older than Kevin, Marissa only 19 months older and Justin 27 months younger. But the siblings were close, despite the frequent arguments when they visited us in New York. I had forgotten how my own boys fought as youngsters. Early on, Kevin started developing unusual and limited eating habits. I'm so grateful he nursed well and long because sometimes I think he stored up all the nutrients that he has excluded from his diet since then! Obviously bright, Kevin started having difficulties at school but it wasn't until years later that he was diagnosed with ADHD. Most teenagers seem incorrigible at times, and Kevin was no exception. He decided to give up baseball, though he played well and his three siblings were immersed in the sport.

Left to right: Tim, Kevin, paternal great-grandmother Mary Mansfield, baby Justin and Marissa in Garden City, N.Y., 2001. *(Photograph courtesy of Dawn Mansfield and published with her permission.)*

Kevin always loved singing, acting, making funnies and Disney World. School only appealed to him when he was engaged in the drama field. His first role in high school was that of LeFou, Gaston's wacky friend in *Beauty and the Beast*. Kevin was perfect for the part, singing, dancing, jumping around the stage. He was hooked! The next year he snagged a starring role in *Shrek,* that of the donkey; his performance was terrific and professional, and of course involved all of his loves. We thought he had finally found his niche, but success was followed by bullying and confrontations that had Kevin in tears and led to his parents' decision to home school him the rest of his senior year. And then…

Early in 2018, I recorded in my journal what unknowingly were very prescient words: "A mother feels a unique pain when each of the children she bore goes through a crisis. I see the reality, I know my children, I witnessed their growth into adulthood and I accept what their life is now. I pray that God grants them the wisdom to see the reality themselves and make wise decisions, none of which I can influence, and me the acceptance of whatever the future holds."

Kevin's older brother Tim was slated to leave for France in late winter to play professional baseball for the Savigny-sur-Orge Lions. Chuck and I offered to fund a trip for the seven of us (Chas, Dawn, Marissa, Kevin, Justin and we) to see him play and manage some side trips to London and Rome. Planning consumed me; at Kevin's insistence we even included a visit to Disney Paris (my eyes rolling at the thought!). When Kevin fell ill, the ensuing crisis made me realize how precious my faith and family are. I could think of little else but the pain in my son's heart. Patience was never his strong suit, but the frustration at not being able to do anything to make his son well was unbearable. I wanted to fly to Charlotte as soon as possible to give a helping hand, but was advised to wait until Kevin's condition stabilized a bit. Undoing the European plans kept me busy until I finally left for Charlotte on March 13th.

Chas picked me up at the airport and we drove straight to the hospital. Kevin was in the process of being transferred from ICU to a step-down unit and my heart stopped when he was wheeled into the room. He couldn't talk or walk, and his six-foot frame showed every ravage of the thirty pounds lost. Tubes protruded from many parts of his body and yet I was assured Kevin was making progress toward a hopefully full recovery. I forced tears away for his sake as I prayed silently that assurances would be fulfilled.

The next week I would label as one of the hardest of my life. Every morning, I would drive in the dark from my sister's house where I was staying to the hospital so that Dawn, who had spent the night there, could go home for a shower and work at the nursery school where she taught four-year olds. (My sister Bernice and husband Bob have lived in Charlotte since 1970. She admitted to me that when she visited Kevin in the hospital in the early days of his hospitalization, she prayed that his parents would not have to make the decision to "pull the plug" on his life-support systems.) Each afternoon, I would go to my son's home to help organize the day-to-day living and receive the food donations that neighbors and friends kept delivering. Every evening I would return to my sister's with a report of the baby steps Kevin was making. The days were as exhausting as I remember when my own children were babies, but I think the psychological demands were worse than the physical ones. Kevin was really trying to respond to the multiple therapies although his fatigue at the slightest exertion was evident. He relished his visitors, mostly family, who kept his spirits up. Being alone was what he feared most. By the time I flew back to Florida a week later, Kevin's speech was somewhat understandable and he was walking with assistance. Chas dropped me at the airport and I no sooner walked through the entry when I completely lost any composure I had maintained, sobbing uncontrollably all the way to the gate.

KEVIN COURAGEOUS

Kevin with Mamie in Charlotte, N.C., spring 2018.
*(Photograph courtesy of Dawn Mansfield and
published with her permission.)*

The next time we saw Kevin was in April, five days before he was released from the hospital. At his first outing from the hospital for a family dinner on Easter Sunday, Chuck toasted the strength and courage Kevin had displayed thus far in his journey toward recovery. Kevin made us smile by his response, "What Kevin are you talking about?" but I think the smiles masked a realization that this boy/man had a longer journey left in which to summon even more.

In the months that followed, there were daily updates about Kevin's condition, but progress slowed. We wanted so desperately for him to be back to "normal" but our impatience would not alter reality. There were times I felt so depressed, but then moments of hope appeared unexpectedly.

While I was proctoring a children's math tournament, one of the visiting teachers shared her story. At age 26, she had just secured a teaching position, and was expecting her first child when she suffered a debilitating stroke. The baby was delivered successfully but the mother's journey back to wellness had just begun. After eighteen months of extensive therapies, hard work and determination, she could concentrate on raising her daughter and once again returned to the classroom, teaching math! She did have some residual effects: her right hand was chronically weak and the graphing piece of the curriculum had to be left largely to an assistant because she couldn't clearly see the boxes on the graph paper. I couldn't wait to share her story with my family.

Even after he had regained various functions, Kevin was still severely vision-impaired in his left eye. The neuro-ophthalmologist in Charlotte gave him little chance of ever regaining the use of the eye, but we didn't want to hear that diagnosis, plain and simple! A good friend recommended a specialist in New York who might see Kevin when his family was visiting in Westhampton, but getting an appointment proved difficult. When we finally received word that Dr. Floyd Warren would see Kevin in less than twenty-four hours, his mother was away visiting her sister, and his father was due to leave the country at the time of the appointment. Still, we were not going to let this opportunity go by, so Chuck, Kevin and I drove into the city, hoping for a different diagnosis. Dr. Warren was wonderful, thorough and, more importantly, optimistic about Kevin's natural ability to heal the eye by resuscitating the damaged brain cells. Kevin really liked the doctor and we were really encouraged by what we heard from him. After the next seven months, Kevin did not need his glasses to avoid the double vision and roving eye conditions that his earlier injuries had caused. Thank you, Dr. Warren, and *Deo gratias*!

Mansclan usually comes to visit us in Westhampton in the summer during which time we could observe the changes and progress Kevin was making. As is often the case with brain injury, Kevin's personality changed slightly; he was a kinder, gentler person, albeit still full of wisecracks. He graciously accepted the help of his family in routine things like cutting meat and carrying objects he feared he might drop. He was totally honest with himself and others about accepting his situation and the hope that therapies would accelerate his recovery. One winter he even ventured to Florida to visit us without his parents, riding with his sister and her boyfriend. I suspect it was the promise of a stop in Disney

World on the way and the ease of avoiding queues with a disability that prompted the visit!

We relish news of any tidbit of progress: a slight decrease in tremors, more articulate speech, activities that get him involved with other young people. Acceptance and gratitude for how far this special man has come mark our days, but do not diminish the hope that Kevin will be able to lead a productive, independent life.

The "Mansclan," as the family is known. Left to right: Chas, Kevin, newborn Justin, Tim, Marissa and Dawn, August 3, 2001.
(Photograph courtesy of Dawn Mansfield and published with her permission.)

The "FAITH OVER FEAR" T-shirt has been widely worn by family and friends since Kevin became ill. The back of the shirt reads: "Baby steps can be taken at any age #allhandsin4kevin". The shirt also comes in blue with orange lettering. *(Photograph courtesy of Dawn Mansfield and published with her permission.)*

A POEM

By Marissa Hope Mansfield

On December 11, 2019, our granddaughter Marissa emailed us as follows: "I was going through old articles and stuff and realized that I never shared this poem with anyone and thought it would be a good addition to the book. Love you always, Marissa."

A good addition indeed. Thank you, Princess.

Her beautiful essay, "Little Brothers Are Worth Everything," appears earlier herein.

There I was
standing with feelings
of guilt and hopelessness.
I was completely in shock.
Everything in my life,
was turning upside down.
Life as I knew it
had changed forever.
Why,
did this happen
to me?
I remember sitting,
waiting for doctors
to tell us any news.
I was in the dark
with no light in sight.
Wires connected,
monitors beeping,
hospital ICU.
The flu sucks.

My brother.
My best friend.
He was lifeless.
He was unconscious.
He was changed.

Marissa and Kevin as "little ones."
*(Photograph courtesy of Dawn Mansfield and
published with her permission.)*

KEVIN

By Kathryn Mary Mansfield

Katie is our daughter, youngest child and Kevin's aunt. A 1996 magna cum laude *alumna of Harvard University who majored in American History, she later received a Master's degree in International Peace Studies from the Kroc Institute at the University of Notre Dame in South Bend, Indiana. She has worked and traveled all over the globe and is currently working at Eastern Mennonite University in Harrisonburg, Virginia, where she serves as a trainer in its STAR (Strategies for Trauma Awareness & Resilience) Program. She is also completing her Ph.D. in Expressive Arts and Conflict Transformation. Following eight years at Goldman Sachs Asset Management, where she became a vice president at age 26, she traveled and worked in many places, including short stints in India and the Philippines, and a three-year stay in Kenya. In her travels she made it to 22,000 feet in the Himalayas, spent time in her maternal grandfather's ancestral Sicily, and jumped out of a perfectly good airplane.*

She wrote the following poem shortly after Kevin fell ill.

Thank you, sweetheart.

Kevin
This loving, sweet, sensitive, curious boy.
Twisting a lock on the top of his head.
Kevin,
This stubborn, brilliant, sensitive, furious boy.
Labeled defiant...
Please take the meds.
Kevin,
This loving, stubborn, sensitive, playful man.
Quieted by fever
Tubed, trapped, in bed.

Kevin,
This loved, prayer-surrounded warrior.
Felt all the love
And returned from the dead!
Kevin,
This writhing, eyes fluttering, hand squeezing fighter.
Beginning anew
All hands in for Kev!
Kevin,
This towering, loving, humorous man.
Continuing to reach
Continuing to teach
Continuing to learn
Continuing to take steps ahead.

I love you, may you continue
To find courage, humor, and creativity
For the journey.

XOXO
Aunt Katie

ANEM NOT AMEN

By Chuck Mansfield

That which does not kill us makes us stronger.

– Friedrich Nietzsche

As my granddaughter Marissa has written earlier herein, ANEM is an abbreviation for Acute Necrotizing Encephalopathy Myelitis. Moreover, she reported, Kevin's illness "is only the second case **EVER** to stem from flu B (the more intense strain)!"*

Based on visits to various websites, here is a primer on ANEM or ANE. The information presented here is intended to inform readers about the severity of Kevin's condition and not to alarm anyone. Not being a medical professional or a scientist, however, the author apologizes in advance for providing perhaps TMI (too much information).

According to my research, neurological complications of influenza have been well documented in medical literature and date from the diagnosis of encephalitis lethargica[1] during the 1918 influenza pandemic.[2] Neurological flu manifestations are now known to include encephalitis, and acute necrotizing encephalopathy (ANE)[3] among other conditions. Reports of ANE began surfacing from Japan during the flu epidemics of the mid- and late 1990s. Flu-associated central nervous system (CNS) dysfunction has also been reported in Europe and the U.S. Other infections associated with ANE include human herpesvirus-6 infection, measles, parainfluenza infection, a very contagious type of viral respiratory infection, and *Mycoplasma* infection, which can cause chronic inflammatory diseases of the respiratory system, urogenital tract, and joints.

According to some Japanese studies, in the most severe cases of flu-associated ANE, patients develop altered mental status with or without seizures and then rapidly progress to a comatose state within a mean of 24–72 hours from the onset of fever and upper respiratory symptoms. This statement is highly consistent with Kevin's horrific experience. Seizures are frequently resistant to antiepileptic medications. Death, which occurs in about 30% of cases, results largely from cardiorespiratory compromise or complications from mechanical ventilation. As written elsewhere herein, at the onset of Kevin's illness medical professionals were seriously concerned and stated that he might not survive.

[1] *According to https://rarediseases.info.nih.gov, "Encephalitis lethargica (EL) is a disease characterized by high fever, headache, double vision, delayed physical and mental response, extreme tiredness (lethargy), and sometimes coma. Patients may also experience abnormal eye movements, upper body weakness, muscle, pain, tremors, neck rigidity, and behavioral changes including psychosis. A worldwide epidemic of EL occurred from 1917 to 1928 with more than one million reported cases. Although occasional cases are reported with similar symptoms, EL epidemics have not recurred. The cause of this condition is unknown, but a viral origin is suspected. Treatment depends on a person's symptoms. Levodopa [one of the main medications used to treat the symptoms of Parkinson's disease] and other antiparkinson drugs may be effective in alleviating some symptoms."*

[2] *According to the U.S. Center for Disease Control and Prevention, "The 1918 influenza pandemic was the most severe pandemic in recent history. It was caused by an H1N1 virus*[4] *with genes of avian origin. Although there is not universal consensus regarding where the virus originated, it spread worldwide during 1918-1919. In the United States, it was first identified in military personnel in spring 1918.*

"It is estimated that about 500 million people or one-third of the world's population became infected with this virus. The number of deaths was estimated to be at least 50 million worldwide with about 675,000 occurring in the United States. Mortality was high in people younger than 5 years old, 20-40 years old, and 65 years and older. The high mortality in

healthy people, including those in the 20-40 year age group, was a unique feature of this pandemic.

"While the 1918 H1N1 virus has been synthesized and evaluated, the properties that made it so devastating are not well understood. With no vaccine to protect against influenza infection and no antibiotics to treat secondary bacterial infections that can be associated with influenza infections, control efforts worldwide were limited to non-pharmaceutical interventions such as isolation, quarantine, good personal hygiene, use of disinfectants, and limitations of public gatherings, which were applied unevenly."

In 2020 the "coronavirus" has made headlines around the world. In a January 27, 2020, op-ed piece in The Wall Street Journal, *Paul Wolfowitz and Max Frost elaborated on the 1918 pandemic:*

"For a precedent, look back to 1918, when the Spanish flu broke out amid World War I. In the U.S., government officials and the press did all they could to play it down lest it hurt the war effort. While the Los Angeles health chief declared there was 'no cause for alarm' and the Arkansas Gazette described the disease as the 'same old fever and chills,' people were dying by the thousands.

"The name 'Spanish flu' was a misnomer. In the countries where it originally surfaced – France, China and the U.S. – the news was suppressed by censorship and self-censorship to maintain wartime morale. (China sent only civilian laborers to the battlefield, but it declared war on Germany in August 1917.) Not until King Alphonse XIII of neutral Spain fell ill did news of the virus spread widely.

"Between the spring of 1918 and early 1919, three waves of Spanish flu tore across the planet, facilitated by censorship and secrecy. The results were catastrophic: 50 million people were killed world-wide, including nearly 700,000 Americans."

[3] *According to https://rarediseases.info.nih.gov, "Acute necrotizing encephalopathy (ANE) is a rare disease characterized by brain damage*

(encephalopathy) that usually follows an acute febrile disease, mostly viral infections. Most of the reported cases are from previously healthy Japanese and Taiwanese children, but it is now known that the disease may affect anybody in the world. The symptoms of the viral infection (fever, respiratory infection, and gastroenteritis, among others) are followed by seizures, disturbance of consciousness that may rapidly progress to a coma, liver problems, and neurological deficits

"*The disease is caused by both environmental factors and genetic factors. Usually, ANE develops secondary to viral infections, among which the influenza A, influenza B, and the human herpes virus 6, are the most common. ANE can be familial or sporadic, but both forms are very similar to each other. Most familial cases are caused by mutations in the RANBP2 gene, and are known as 'infection-induced acute encephalopathy 3 (IIAE3).'*

"*Although the clinical course and the prognosis of ANE are diverse, the characteristic that is specific to the disease is the 'multifocal symmetric brain lesions affecting the thalami, brain stem, cerebral white matter, and cerebellum' which can be seen on computed tomography (CT) or magnetic resonance imaging (MRI) exams. A picture of the brain may help you better visualize the areas of the brain affected. The best treatment of ANE is still under investigation but may include corticosteroids [steroid hormones that are either produced by the body or are manmade] and anticytokine [treatment by interference with the function of cytokines, such as tumor necrosis factor, an inflammatory cytokine involved in the pathogenesis of rheumatoid arthritis therapies], including TNFα antagonists. [5]*"

[4] "*H1N1 flu is also known as swine flu . It's called swine flu because in the past, the people who caught it had direct contact with pigs. That changed several years ago, when a new virus emerged that spread among people who hadn't been near pigs.*

"*In 2009, H1N1 was spreading fast around the world, so the World Health Organization called it a pandemic. Since then, people have continued to get sick from swine flu, but not as many.*"

[5] *According to www.sciencedirect.com, "TNFα antagonists are effective in the treatment of chronic inflammatory joint disease. Despite a good*

overall safety profile, they can induce a number of adverse effects, including autoimmunity and infections. A link between TNFα antagonists and vasculitides[6] *has been suggested."*

[6] *According to www.amboss.com, "Vasculitides are a heterogeneous group of autoimmune diseases, all characterized by inflammation of blood vessels (vasculitis) and subsequent ischemia [According to www.webmd.com, "Ischemia is a serious problem where some part of your body, like your heart or brain, isn't getting enough blood.] and damage to the organs supplied by these vessels. Vasculitis may occur as a primary disease (idiopathic) or as a secondary response to an underlying disease (e.g., hepatitis B infection). Based on the size of the vessel affected, it can be classified into small-vessel, medium-vessel, or large-vessel vasculitis. While the inflammatory process may be confined to one organ, it may also involve several organ systems. Vasculitis should be considered in patients presenting with palpable purpura [purple-colored spots most recognizable on the skin], pulmonary infiltrates, unexplained ischemic events, and multisystem disease. The detection of antineutrophil cytoplasmic antibodies* [7] *(ANCA) in the blood is an important diagnostic marker; however, there are also ANCA-negative vasculitis syndromes. Immunosuppressive treatment is administered to stop vascular inflammation. Specific (e.g., antiviral drugs) or symptomatic (e.g., NSAID [nonsteroidal anti-inflammatory drugs]) management may be necessary. If the vasculitis is secondary to an underlying disease, treatment of the underlying disease should be initiated."*

[7] *According to www.en.wikipedia.com, "Anti-neutrophil cytoplasmic antibodies (ANCAs) are a group of autoantibodies, mainly of the IgG [Immunoglobulin G] type, against antigens in the cytoplasm [the contents outside of the nucleus and enclosed within the membrane of a cell] of neutrophil granulocytes (the most common type of white blood cell) and monocytes [the largest cells in the blood]. They are detected as a blood test in a number of autoimmune disorders, but are particularly associated with systemic vasculitis, so called ANCA-associated vasculitides (AAV)."* (Authors' note: Aren't you glad you asked?)

According to https://ghr.nlm.nih.gov, "Acute necrotizing encephalopathy type 1, also known as susceptibility to infection-induced acute encephalopathy 3 or IIAE3, is a rare type of brain disease (encephalopathy) that occurs following a viral infection such as the flu.

"Acute necrotizing encephalopathy type 1 typically appears in infancy or early childhood, although some people do not develop the condition until adolescence or adulthood. People with this condition usually show typical symptoms of an infection, such as fever, cough, congestion, vomiting, and diarrhea, for a few days. Following these flu-like symptoms, affected individuals develop neurological problems, such as seizures, hallucinations, difficulty coordinating movements (ataxia), or abnormal muscle tone. Eventually, most affected individuals go into a coma, which usually lasts for a number of weeks. The condition is described as 'acute' because the episodes of illness are time-limited." This is, of course, exactly what happened to Kevin, although he was comatose for only seven days and showed significant improvement overall in just three weeks.

"People with acute necrotizing encephalopathy type 1 develop areas of damage (lesions) in certain regions of the brain. As the condition progresses, these brain regions develop swelling (edema), bleeding (hemorrhage), and then tissue death (necrosis). The progressive brain damage and tissue loss results in encephalopathy." Again, this is what happened to Kevin.

"Approximately one-third of individuals with acute necrotizing encephalopathy type 1 do not survive their illness and subsequent neurological decline. [This "one-third" mortality statistic is consistent with the information Kevin's medical professionals and caregivers provided early in his ordeal.] Of those who do survive, about half have permanent brain damage due to tissue necrosis, resulting in impairments in walking, speech, and other basic functions. [This, alas, was also consistent with Kevin's condition and prognosis.] Over time, many of these skills may be regained, but the loss of brain tissue is permanent. Other individuals who survive their illness appear to recover completely.

"It is estimated that half of individuals with acute necrotizing encephalopathy type 1 are susceptible to recurrent episodes and will have another infection that results in neurological decline; some people may have numerous episodes throughout their lives. Neurological function worsens following each episode as more brain tissue is damaged."

Although Kevin has been designated "completely and permanently disabled," the fact that he has survived his tragic illness against daunting odds and made positive – some would say, miraculous – progress, has given us all ongoing hope that he will "recover completely."

(Courtesy of the U.S. National Library of Medicine)

* *According to www.en.wikipedia.com, "Myelitis is inflammation of the spinal cord which can disrupt the normal responses from the brain to the rest of the body, and from the rest of the body to the brain. Inflammation in the spinal cord, can cause the myelin and axon [8] to be damaged resulting in symptoms such as paralysis and sensory loss. Myelitis is classified to several categories depending on the area or the cause of the lesion; however, any inflammatory attack on the spinal cord is often referred to as transverse myelitis."*

[8] According to www.en.wikipedia.com, "Myelin is a lipid-rich (fatty) substance that surrounds nerve cell axons (the nervous system's wires) to insulate them and increase the rate at which information (encoded as electrical impulses) is passed along the axon. The myelinated axon can be likened to an electrical wire (the axon) with insulating material (myelin) around it."

HAVE I LOST MY MIND?

By Dawn Chiaramonte Mansfield
With Illustrations by Jane Tronco

KEVIN COURAGEOUS

Kevin was a happy Kangaroo. He could be found singing and hopping around the zoo all day long.

He would tell the silliest jokes and Kevin liked to imitate the other animals. The animals loved when Kevin would come to visit and impersonate them. It made them feel so special.

One day after Kevin woke up, he saw Charlie Cow over by the barn. Kevin tried to, "Moo," but it sounded more like, "Hoo!" Charlie just shook his head and said, "I think you have lost your mind Kevin. "I do not sound like an owl. Kevin shrugged, cleared his throat and hopped away.

Later, he bumped into Timmy Tiger. Kevin was sure he could do this but, instead of letting out a big, "Roar," he just started to snore. Timmy's face said it all. "You must have lost your mind Kevin. That was not a Roar'" Timmy said. Kevin thought this was weird but, he did not let it bother him.

Just in the hen house, Kevin saw Conner Chicken. "I know I can get this one right," Kevin said softly. As he went to let out a big, "Cluck!" all that popped out of his mouth was a tiny, "Coo."

Finally, Kevin passed by Marissa Monkey. He was very excited to show her his imitation. He had been working really hard on this one and was sure he could do it. He took a deep breath and tried to let out a loud, "Oo Oo Ah Ah!" but all that came out was, "Meow." Marissa stopped in her tracks and stared at Kevin. "Have you totally lost your mind Kevin? I do not sound like a cat."

This continued to happen as he ran into all of his friends. The animals were all beginning to laugh at Kevin now. He was making all the wrong sounds, but why? "Maybe I have lost my mind," Kevin thought.

So off he went to find it but, "Where does one look for a lost mind?" he thought.

After looking all over the zoo with no luck, Kevin was tired and fell asleep. Finally, right there in the middle of his dream, was his mind, just where he had left it.

The next morning, Kevin woke up to all his friends surrounding him. "What are you all doing here?" he asked. "You have been talking in your sleep all morning. Your impersonation's have been awesome!" roared Timmy the Tiger. "We voted your imitation of Marissa Monkey as the best," clucked Conner Chicken. "We were getting worried about you", said Marissa. "We all thought you had lost your mind."

Nope, thought Kevin,
"I knew where it was all along!"

MESSAGES FROM AN AMPUTEE FRIEND

By Brian Maher

Brian is a retired college administrator, writer and involved Catholic who is married to Barbara Goble Maher, Mame's Garden City High School classmate and Chuck's sweetheart of yesteryear. His kindness and concern are amply demonstrated in his prayers for Kevin and when he checks in from time to time to ask how Kevin is doing, as in the following recent examples.

> *...and the hills and valleys of life continue for us all. The keys are to recognize the balance in our lives, to be grateful for the many blessings we have been given, and to fight through the times which are not so great.*
>
> – Brian Maher

Though never so diagnosed, I was technically disabled since the day I was born, and it became official when my leg was amputated at age 30.

Like Sully, John Devine, and many more, I almost wore my condition as a badge of honor and realized I had the opportunity to have a positive effect on other people's lives.

Once Kevin gets it, he will do the same.

Chuck's comments follow.

Brian Maher's 110 words above are inspirational and contain lessons for us all.

"Sully" and John Devine are both friends of Brian's (and mine) and profiles in courage of the highest order. Indeed, as you will read below, both have been one-legged phenomena!

Sully is George R. Sullivan, who passed away on January 9, 2020, following a long battle with daunting medical conditions including a heart attack, pneumonia and related complications. He was an epic friend of more than 53 years and a fellow Marine who lost a leg in combat, sustained multiple other gunshot wounds during the Vietnam War and was awarded the Navy Cross, second only to the Congressional Medal of Honor, for valor, the citation for which follows:

"The President of the United States of America takes pleasure in presenting the Navy Cross to First Lieutenant George R. Sullivan (MCSN: 0-94356), United States Marine Corps Reserve, for extraordinary heroism while serving as a Platoon Commander with Company L, Third Battalion, Fourth Marines, THIRD Marine Division (Reinforced), Fleet Marine Force, in the Republic of Vietnam on 17 March 1967 during Operation PRAIRIE II. While on a search and clear mission in the vicinity of Dong Ha in the Quang Tri Province, Second Lieutenant Sullivan's platoon was approaching a suspected Viet Cong controlled village when it came under intense small arms and automatic weapons fire from a well concealed enemy force of estimated battalion size. After skillfully employing his men in order to bring a heavy volume of fire on the enemy positions, Second Lieutenant Sullivan observed an enemy automatic weapon to his front and realizing the necessity of neutralizing the well-fortified position, he courageously moved across open fire-swept terrain to within ten meters of the Viet Cong emplacement and silenced the enemy weapon with a grenade. After he had directed a machine gun team into a forward position to deliver suppressive fire at the enemy, he observed that the team's weapon had malfunctioned. Unhesitatingly he moved through concentrated enemy fire to the team's location and cleared the weapon. Meanwhile, another machine gun team had begun moving their weapon forward, but both Marines were wounded and fell in an area exposed to enemy fire. Courageously, Second Lieutenant Sullivan again disregarded the heavy enemy fire and unmindful of his own personal safety, moved to their position and carried them to a defiladed area, undoubtedly saving their lives. Later, while moving among his men, encouraging them and directing their fire, he was painfully wounded in his shoulder, arm and both legs. Although unable to move, he continued to direct the actions of his platoon while requesting air support, medical evacuation for the wounded and a resupply of ammunition, and only after reinforcements had arrived, under the cover of darkness, did he allow himself to be evacuated. By his intrepid fighting spirit, selfless courage, bold initiative and unswerving devotion to duty at great personal risk, Second Lieutenant Sullivan reflected great credit upon himself, and upheld the highest traditions of the Marine Corps and the United States Naval Service."

Many of Sully's fellow Marine officers strongly believe that his valorous actions in combat during which he sustained such ghastly and painful wounds actually merited an award of the Medal of Honor. Alas, our beloved Marine Corps has a reputation for conservatism in awarding such extraordinary military decorations.

After his traumatic injuries, Sully spent over a year in various hospitals. The first time I saw him after I got back from Vietnam was, I believe, in 1973 in Westhampton Beach, New York, where I live during the warm weather. My sons, Chas, then five years old, John, three, and I were walking on the beach and came upon several young adults playing volleyball in the sand. One of the young men in the game was jumping around *on one leg*! It was Sully. I led my sons to meet him and he said, "Boys, come with me; I want to show you something." He then hopped to a nearby blanket where he unveiled his prosthetic leg, which he proceeded to attach. The little guys' jaws dropped!

As New York State Senator Kenneth LaValle has written, "Mr. Sullivan's war injury did not deter him in the slightest, as is evident in his many successful pursuits following his military career." Indeed, Sully went on to become a certified public accountant (CPA), be awarded an MBA (Master of Business Administration), found and lead his own accounting firm and become a near-scratch golfer. He had still served as Receiver of Taxes for the Town of Southold, Long Island, although he did not run for reelection in November 2019 after many years in the office. I had lunch with him on October 15, 2019. It was the last time I saw him.

George Sullivan pictured at his Southold, N.Y., home in 2017.
*(Photograph courtesy of The Suffolk Times and
republished with its permission.
Credit: The Suffolk Times, Joe Werkmeister)*

I shared Sully's story with Kevin. Indeed, Sully is a genuine hero and not just because of his Navy Cross. No, it is because he never gave up on life or felt sorry for himself despite, like Kevin, a 100% disability and strong odds against his long-term well-being. I have known him since 1966 and there is no human being I admire and respect more. He has also written a chapter in my *VIETNAM* book, which is entitled "A Successful Life."

This is where Kevin comes in. I admire and respect him just as much for who and what he is—and the great potential he has. He has a keen intellect, is highly articulate and possesses an extraordinary sense of humor. Moreover, he knows that his grandmother and I are working on this book entitled *KEVIN COURAGEOUS: A Journey of Faith, Hope and Love*, for that courage is what is needed and Kevin has been seeking since he emerged from that coma some two years ago; and I believe he can and will tap into it. To me, like Sully, he has all the ability, grit and strength of character necessary to meet the challenges ahead and succeed in life. Many others, including his grandparents, will do whatever they can for him but, in the last analysis, the outcome of his young life, like Sully's, is all up to him. In this connection, I commended to Kevin the classic poem "Invictus," which is Latin for "unconquered," by the great English poet William Ernest Henley. In the poem the speaker proclaims his strength in the face of adversity, and its last two lines are: "I am the master of my fate, / I am the captain of my soul." *(Authors' note: The poem appears in its entirety near the end of this work.)*

Shortly before noon on December 26, 2019, I received the last email I would receive from Sully. In it he wrote, "Chuck, I feel like the end is near and just want to thank you for your friendship over the years. Sully"

Sully's wake and Mass of Christian Burial were held, respectively, on January 14 and 15, 2020, near his home in Southold, N.Y. He will be interred with full military honors at Arlington National Cemetery.

Godspeed and *Semper fi*, Sully.

Like Sully, John Devine is another friend, Marine Corps veteran and combat amputee, who received Purple Heart and Navy Commendation Medals for his service in the Vietnam War. He and Sully were the closest of friends.

According to an interview by [then-student] Yosef Borenstein at shs.touro.edu, "As a teenager, Mr. Devine was an athlete and swim champion—'his whole life ahead of him.' ... At age eighteen, he joined the Marine Corps, was flown to Vietnam, and then suddenly—only twenty-six days after he was deployed—he became an amputee from the war. [Like Kevin] 'He had to learn everything over again, from walking, to what he's going to do for the rest of his life.' But Mr. Devine, Yosef learned, didn't let this stop him—he told his mother, the first time she saw him after he returned home: 'Mom, no more crying—the crying is over with. I don't know how I'm going to do this, but I'm going to pull it off. The only tears from here on will be tears of joy.'

Not only did he begin walking again, but also took up skiing, bowling, harmonica, ukulele, golf, and, yes, swimming competitively. He only used a wheelchair once in his life—during a 1985 Vietnam Veterans [New York City Welcome Home] street parade. He's visited Walter Reed/Bethesda about forty times to speak, and give encouragement to, veterans from Iraq and Afghanistan.

"'The interview definitely made me understand the life of an amputee better, and the extreme challenges they face,' said Yosef, reflecting on the experience. 'It's not always the disability itself that's most challenging; sometimes it's facing the crowd again…for example, I was surprised to hear that when he began swimming competitively for the first time again, the hardest part wasn't swimming with one leg, it was getting from the car to the pool while everyone was staring.'"

Lance Corporal John Devine, USMC, with his mother Margaret at the Brooklyn Navy Yard in October 1968 for the awarding of his Navy Commendation Medal.
(Photograph by the late Jim Ruth, courtesy of John Devine and published with his permission.)

Here is the citation that accompanied John's Navy Commendation Medal:

"For heroic achievement while serving as a Scout with Company A, First Reconnaissance Battalion, First Marine Division in connection with operations against insurgent communist (Viet Cong) forces in the Republic of Vietnam. On 26 April 1968, Private First Class DEVINE was a member of a reconnaissance patrol which had established a roving observation post in Quang Nam Province. While he was standing watch at a machine gun position which commanded a heavily used trail, the patrol's defensive position came under heavy enemy mortar fire, killing one Marine and wounding five others, including Private First Class DEVINE. Despite extremely serious and painful fragmentation wounds to his legs, which subsequently resulted in the loss of his right leg, Private First Class DEVINE remained alert to a possible enemy ground attack and offered words of comfort and encouragement to the other casualties until he was medically evacuated. His courage, professionalism and sincere concern for the welfare of his comrades were an inspiration to all who observed him. By his exemplary leadership, unwavering determination and selfless devotion to duty, Private First Class DEVINE upheld the finest traditions of the Marine Corps and of the United States Naval Service.

"Private First Class DEVINE is authorized to wear the Combat 'V'."

Semper fidelis, John.

A MONTH OF EMAILS

By Mary Ann and Chuck Mansfield

We get letters. We get letters, stacks and stacks of letters.

– The Perry Como Show

By our count 270 emails from some 120 individuals, "Kevin's Prayer Warriors," were received by Chuck alone in the first month following the onset of Kevin's illness on February 23, 2018. That's an average of almost ten emails per day. Because of sheer numbers and the similarity of sentiments communicated in many of the messages, which filled 57 pages, we have selected those that have struck us as the most meaningful.

It is no surprise that during this period Kevin's mother Dawn was the most prolific messenger. Indeed, her performance, as written elsewhere herein, was heroic. Still, the sheer number of emails conveying good wishes and commitments of prayers for Kevin and his recovery were epic and profoundly inspirational. We share these heartfelt messages with readers here.

February 24th

From Dawn Chiaramonte Mansfield:

Kevin is at Presby Main in the Neuro ICU. His condition is critical but stable. He tested positive for the flu but has post infection encephalitis. His CT scan and MRI both showed swelling and lesions on his brain. His temperature went up to 103.7 last night. He is hooked up to an EEG to monitor his brain waves to make sure there are no seizures. They took him off the sedative a few hours ago to evaluate him. He is responding some by moving his hands. I can see in his eyes that he is scared as we all are. We will keep you posted as we know more but please keep those prayers going. Hug your babies today!

MARY ANN AND CHUCK MANSFIELD

Kevin, circa age 10, with his Mom.
(Photograph courtesy of Chas Mansfield and published with his permission.)

From cousin Megan Mansfield, daughter of Chuck's late godfather, Joseph F. Mansfield:
  Oh my goodness! What a terrible situation. Please let me know if we can do anything for you. I am going to 5:00 Mass so prayers are forthcoming!

From Christina and Bain Slack, friend, former Marine, Vietnam War veteran and combat helicopter pilot:
  I was shocked to hear about your grandson's illness. Please be certain that Christina and I both are praying for his swift and complete recovery. Although his symptoms are very serious, please be advised that modern medicine is capable of accomplishing miracles on a routine and daily basis. Kevin is in a good medical facility and I am sure that he is receiving the best of care. I am living proof of the modern medical miracles that our doctors and nurses are able to do. They saved me after I was nearly dead. Tell Mame and your entire family that we are praying for them and Kevin, with all the power of prayer that we can summon.

From Linda Giarraputo Jeans, a friend and Mame's high-school classmate:
  Prayers are with your grandson. I have forwarded his name and condition to my prayer circle. I can only imagine the anguish you all are

feeling. We know the power of prayer, the human spirit and youth. That is a powerful combination; hope is comforting. God's healing touch upon Kevin.

From Patty and Bob Lund, Chuck's college classmate, fellow Marine and friend of nearly 58 years; Chuck introduced Patty, whom he's known even longer, to Bob in 1964:

We hope things are improving and can't imagine what the whole family is enduring. We're only a little over three hours away. If we can help in any way, let us know.

From Peggy Mansfield, Chuck's sister:

We are all worried and heartbroken that Kevin is going through this horror. I can only imagine what you, Mame and the Mansclan are experiencing. I know that there are tons of people sending good thoughts your way. Kevin is healthy and strong and will get through this with all of you loving him.

Please know that all of us here in Ventura are sending our love.

From Janice and Larry Hennessy, lifelong friends; Larry was a groomsman in our wedding party:

That is awful news about your grandson, Kevin. But being young he has a good chance of recovering 100%. I know how you must feel but you can be certain that we will keep him in our prayers every day. Please give Chas and his wife, Dawn, our best and the whole family for that matter. Be strong!!!

February 25th

From Art Burns, Chuck's college classmate and friend of nearly 58 years:

Terribly sorry to hear this news. Just a short note here to let you and Mame know that you and your grandson are very much in our thoughts and prayers. Please keep me posted if you can. Dedicated rehab and your loving family support will do wonders. Keep the faith!

February 26th

From Lucine Marous, a friend who completed her late husband John's memoir after his passing:

Almost by accident I found your report and was comforted to hear that things are quiet. Of course our prayers for you all will continue. And let's not forget that when doctors explain possible complications, etc., we also know that youthfulness can skew the possible outcomes in a strongly positive way. Here's hoping. Good night/morning and God bless.

From Donna and John Webster, Chuck's college classmate and friend of almost 58 years:

Thanks for the update on Kevin's condition. We have been praying for his complete recovery and he is constantly in our thoughts. Love to all the Mansfields.

From Chuck/Dad/Poppa/Uncle Chunk:

Most of you know that my grandson Kevin, 18, my son Chas' second son, was hospitalized last Friday with flu-related encephalitis. Chas called this morning and reported little change in Kevin's condition, although he tested negative for meningitis. Kevin is moving more but the movement is largely involuntary as he is mostly asleep. However, he was able to deliver a "double thumbs up" when requested to do so, so that's a plus. Chas said Kevin also moved his feet as if he were about to get out of bed. Again the progress is very slow and it is still not known when Kevin will begin his rehabilitation therapies.

Thank you all for the prayers and good wishes. It is amazingly comforting to have family members and friends who care so deeply. Please keep the prayers coming.

May God bless you and your loved ones.

From a family member:
Hi Chuck,

Thanks for update. It's a tough time for all. I myself have cried about Kevin, and I know the sadness about this must be even worse for you and Mame, his beloved grandparents.

Please let us know if you hear any more news. Hoping to hear soon that Kevin has awakened.

From Very Reverend Jude Peters, Chuck's first cousin:
Dear Chuck & Mame,

Just wanted you to know that Carmelites all over the world are praying for Kevin. I offered Mass for his intentions yesterday. Be assured of our continued prayers. Love & prayer.

From Joanne and Roger Hunt, former Marine, Vietnam War veteran, combat helicopter pilot, Chuck's college classmate and friend of nearly 58 years:
Dear Chuck & Mame,

Thank you so much for the update. We are keeping Kevin, you both, and all your family in our daily prayers. When our granddaughter Taylor was diagnosed three years ago, at age five, with brain cancer, we were all obviously devastated. Chad taught us to keep focused on the positive. Her team of doctors was the best in their fields at Children's National Hospital in DC. And they started her on chemotherapy immediately. Now, even though her tumor is larger than her eyeball, it is stable - the best news we can hope for. We stay focused on the positive. I hope you both can focus on the positive. The test for meningitis was negative. Kevin is making progress, even though slowly. He gave the thumbs up sign. He moved his feet ...... You want and need to be strong for Kevin, Chas, Dawn, his siblings. Focusing on the positives will give you strength, as well as all the prayers from your family and friends. Our hearts go out to you all.

From Bro. Thomas J. Cleary, S.M., President of Chaminade High School (Mineola, N.Y.):

Prayers from the Marianists (Society of Mary) continue for Kevin.

From Bain Slack:

Chuck: This is wonderful news. The fact that he is moving in his sleep means that his brain is making a comeback toward relearning the natural physical acts of everyday life. He will come back from this, I am sure of it.

It may take some time and it may take a lot of effort, but these early signs indicate that he can make a full recovery and live a full life. Remember also, that an 18 year old is capable of amazing things that we old dogs could never accomplish.

Christina and I are totally excited by this news. It is great. Thank God.

February 27th

From Denis M. Murphy, M.D., Mame's first boyfriend in Garden City, Chuck's mother's "third son," Chuck's college roommate, a former Air Force officer, a charter member of the Rinkachous of America since 1957* and family friend for almost 68 years:
Dear Chuck and Mame,

Just got your e-mail. So sorry to hear about Kevin. We all pray for his recovery and the suffering that you and Mame are going through. Please keep me informed as his progress continues.
Love, Murph

* For fuller perspective please see "Kevin Sean Mansfield, R.O.A." later herein.

From Kelli Hall of Federated Hermes, Inc.:
Hi Mr. & Mrs. Mansfield,

I am sorry to hear about Kevin and his condition and I pray that he continues to give the double thumbs up and recovers with no brain damage or any other damage. How incredibly scary this is and I can't imagine what you are going through. My prayer is that the Lord will heal him from the inside and make him healthy and strong. Please keep us all updated on his condition as we all pray will be better news. In my prayers and thoughts.

From Dawn Chiaramonte Mansfield:

So today had its ups and downs. Kevin has been moving his arms around more today. He has a stubborn streak, in case you didn't know. He had to be re-intubated because he bit a hole in his tube. They have figured out that it is a viral infection not bacterial.

The second CT scan came back today. No change in the swelling and a little more blood showing in the Thalamus part of the brain. They plan on doing another MRI and spinal tap later in the week. Keep those prayers coming. I can feel the love!

From Joe Sullivan and family:

Chuck, prayers will start immediately. Daily during the week I visit my city church to pray and today I will make another trip. Before Shane converted from Buddhism I used to say one Catholic and two Buddhist prayers for you. Now I can say two Catholics and one Buddhist. Susie's prayers are very powerful and she also prays daily. Kevin and his family will be in our prayers. God bless!

From Therese Mikulus, a friend and Chaminade Mom:

I'm so sorry all of this is happening. I was up most of the night praying for many things and of course Kevin is at the top of my list. I believe in the power of prayer and I know there are hundreds of us praying for his recovery. God always listens and He is sure to hear all of us.

I will continue to pray. Big hug to you.

From Tom Kiley, Chuck's Chaminade and Holy Cross classmate and teammate, essayist and friend of nearly 62 years:

Thanks, Chuck. He is strong and in his youth and prime. With prayer and Our Lord's intercession, he will pull through. I believe that.

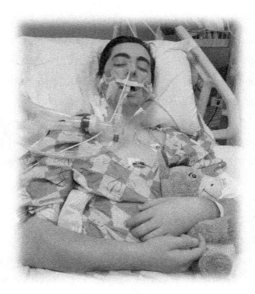

Kevin comatose.
Note Donkey in the lower right corner.
*(Photograph courtesy of Dawn Mansfield and
published with her permission.)*

From Lori and Rich Hensler; Lori is Treasurer of Federated Hermes, Inc., on whose board Chuck has served for twenty-one years; Rich is her husband:

I just saw the note from Dee (Marley, Federated Hermes, Inc.) regarding your grandson Kevin's illness and current condition. What a shock it was to read these updates. Please know that Rich and I are praying for Kevin's full and speedy recovery. He is in the best possible place for these things to transpire. Still, we are sending positive and healing thoughts across the miles. Kevin, you, Mame, your son and his family are all in our thoughts and prayers and if there is anything we can do for all of you, please let us know. Take good care.

From Joanne and Roger Hunt:

Thank you for the update. Dawn is amazing; keeping strong through this nightmare and so considerate to keep all her family & friends informed of

all the latest developments. She must be so exhausted emotionally, mentally, & physically, as we know you all are.
Love and prayers.

February 28th

From Mary Ann Mansfield:
I feel like we take one step forward, two steps back but as long as we hear one positive thing each day we are grateful. Yesterday they did a chest scan. We didn't find out till later on that Kevin has pneumonia. Not great but totally expected since he has the flu. Horrible to watch anyone cough with a breathing tube down their throat. Even in the condition he is in, he is still trying to get that tube out. He has now put a hole in the cup located in his throat. They will do everything possible to work around it so they won't have to re-intubate him...AGAIN! Chest x-ray taken a little while ago showed some improvement regarding pneumonia.

From family members:
Thank you, Chuck. We have been keeping a picture of Kevin and sibs on our dining room table with a candle next to it. Like a little altar I guess. But we don't need the picture and candle to remind us...I am thinking of him the whole time, as I know you must be. Let's hope he will turn a corner soon.

From Bob Meikle, Chuck's college classmate and friend of nearly 58 years:
This must be truly agonizing for you all. Will continue to pray for a turn for the best and Kevin's eventual recovery. Love to all.

From Barbara and Tom Kiley:
Dear Chuck and Mame,
We are upset to learn of Kevin's pneumonia but we have faith that this too shall pass. He is a strong young man and will respond to the antibiotics. Just want you to know that my (Our Lady of Mercy Academy) friends are praying for him, his parents and you and they have passed his name along

to their prayer groups. Our friends are like the stars - we don't always see them but they are always there. We are grateful for your updates and hope you can feel our prayers and thoughts. You are never out of our thoughts. We will dedicate our First Friday Rosary to Kevin at OLMA. Love you both.

From Anke Muench (Augsburg, Germany):

For Dawn, from one mother to another mother: I can't imagine what you must be going through. I am feeling with you and my mother's heart is sending out love and strength for you and your family. I will keep on praying for your Kevin.

Remember all those balloons in the car in Westhampton nine years ago this summer? Love.

From Ed Matthews, Chuck's college classmate, fellow Marine, Vietnam War veteran and friend of nearly 58 years:

Chuck: Your daughter-in-law has a great attitude and approach during very difficult circumstances. It is difficult when we are dealing with medical/health issues affecting our children. When our Ted had his head injury and was in a coma for two weeks it was difficult but each positive sign is uplifting. It is hard to not let the backwards step discourage you. We will continue our prayers.

From Bain Slack:

Chuck: It is going to be a hard slow process for him to fully recover. It may be painful to watch sometimes. But the main thing is that he will make it!!! Being 18 years old gives the young man a huge strength and resiliency to draw upon and those traits will be the keys to his recovery.

You tell Mame and all of your family just to be patient, have faith and stick with Kevin and together you will see him pull through and return to the young man he was before this illness struck. We are praying for Kevin and all of you.

March 1ˢᵗ

From Chuck:
My son Chas called this morning with "good news." He reported that last evening a nurse prompted Kevin to squeeze her hands and wiggle his toes, which he did. Chas was thrilled when Kevin partially opened his eyes, the first time since this all began that Chas has witnessed that.

Amazingly, Kevin is only the second known case of this particular strain of flu-induced encephalitis. Now Kevin will receive a drug that will be a form of chemotherapy to help offset the threats now caused by his immune system. Chas indicated that the brain swelling is down and the brain lesions are diminished, which are positive developments.

Kevin's Mom, Dawn, posted the following on Facebook:
"Lots of emotions today. To start, Kevin's MRI came back today and the swelling and the bleeding have decreased some. He had to have his intubation tube re-inserted AGAIN. Kevin's official diagnosis will probably make him a case study as he is only the 2ⁿᵈ documented case to ever have Acute Necrotizing Encephalopathy Myelitis, which is a direct result of the Flu Strain B. His immune system is attacking the membranes of the nerves in his brain.

"They will be starting a procedure tomorrow called Plasmapheresis. This is very similar to dialysis. They are also going to start giving him a chemo drug to help calm down the immune system. We have a long road ahead of us. Keep praying, PLEASE!"

Please continue your prayers for Kevin and his family.

From Rev. John Worthley, Chuck's Chaminade and Holy Cross classmate and friend of almost 62 years:
Dear Chuck and Mame,
So glad for the good news. Prayers continued. I remember Kevin so well from your 50ᵗʰ anniversary Mass. All shall be well!

From Kay and Doyce Payne; Florida friends, Kay is a retired R.N. and Doyce, her husband, a retired M.D.:

Chuck,

This is indeed, good news!! So thankful for the therapies which can be used to treat the brain injury. We will pray for an excellent response to these and for continued improvement.

Our God is faithful!!

Love & Prayers.

From Brian Maher, whose inspirational words, including "A Message from an Amputee Friend," appear earlier herein:
Chuck:
I put Kevin's name in the book of intentions at 7:45 Mass this morning. He'll get a decade of the Rosary later today.
Keep me posted.
Blessings.

March 2<u>nd</u>

Facebook posting by Dawn Chiaramonte Mansfield:
We found out that Kevin does not have pneumonia. His coughing is coming from a combination of him having had the flu and a gag reflex from his breathing tube. First thing this morning Kevin had a Quinton catheter (central line) put in his neck. He had the first of four of his Plasmapheresis procedures. This procedure takes out the blood, removes all the impurities and then puts it back with new generated plasma. Each procedure will take about two hours. He got to rest the remainder of the day, something he hasn't gotten to do in six.

The Mansclan [Chas and Dawn's family] would like to thank you for all your prayers, messages, visits, calls, and meals. You really don't realize just how big your village is until something like this happens. It's going to be a long road ahead and we are so blessed to have wonderful support along the way.

From Lucine Marous:
Dear One,
Mame was on my mind today simply because I know how much easier the rough patches are when we are sharing them with a loved one, and you

couldn't be there to take part, but she sounded as though she is using her resources to get her through this one.

March 3rd

Facebook posting by Dawn Chiaramonte Mansfield:

We thought we might have had to re-re-re-intubate again today since Kevin pushed his tube out again but they were able to fix it. Kevin had his second treatment today. They said they are hoping to see some improvement with each one. Well, we saw it. Kevin is now in what they call an encephalopathic state which means he is in and out of consciousness due to his diminished mental state. That said, he has opened his eyes three different times today and responded to given commands (hand squeezes and toe wiggles) each time. He is completely distraught each time he wakes up and gags himself into a coughing fit which causes his vitals to escalate. All that aside we are thrilled with today's progress.

March 5th

Facebook posting by Dawn Chiaramonte Mansfield:

This morning's dilemma. Do they keep Kevin's breathing tube in and keep sedating him with higher dosages because he keeps gagging/coughing and getting very agitated? Do they take the tube out and hope that he is completely able to breathe without any difficulties? THEY TOOK THE TUBE OUT!!! So far so good. He was awake most of the evening and following commands with his hands. He has a lot to cough up but as long as he can do that through the night the tube will hopefully be history. It may be a long road ahead but the view just got a whole lot brighter!

From Mary Ann Mansfield:

Again, thank you for your prayers and loving support. If any of you are inclined, friends have set up a gofundme page for the astronomical costs of weeks-long hospitalization and even longer rehabilitation. The website is gofundme.com, then search for Kevin Mansfield.

March 6th

Facebook posting by Dawn Chiaramonte Mansfield:
　　We have been overwhelmed by the prayers, support and love that has come from friends, family and acquaintances around the world. You are the fingers of God's hands as He holds Kevin and us in His palms. Chas has said that he will spend the rest of his life paying forward to others the kindness we have been shown. Keep it coming!

　　Kevin had a huge, exhausting day! He received his fifth and final Plasmapheresis treatment early. Around 10 am, the Nurse Practitioner, Erica, gave him a neurological exam. He raised his arms at the elbow. He held his arms a short while off the bed from the shoulder. He stuck out his tongue. He gave Erica a high five and raised his legs 6-8 inches to "kick" her hands. The nurses, Erica and Chas were sooo excited, and Kevin gave a little fist pump and said in a very raspy voice, "I did it!" At the same time, he had a big smile on his face, and tears of joy were streaming down his face. It was like something out of a Rocky movie.

　　He was not finished! With physical therapists' assistance, he sat up on the side of the bed, stood up and sat in a chair. He spent a few hours in a recliner OUT OF THE BED. Then he was finished. He spent most of the afternoon near catatonic, but closed the day with a good neuro exam by the doctor after a nap.

　　Please keep him and us in your prayers as these are tremendous baby steps, but he has a long way to go. He still has a feeding tube, his eyes are still not quite working together, he cannot yet support his own weight, and he still struggles to communicate anything with complexity. None of that changes how far he has come though, and the fact that today, he is further along than doctors told us to expect.

March 7th

CaringBridge posting by Dawn Chiaramonte Mansfield:
　　Kevin had another productive and exhausting day! He had visits from his PT (physical therapist) and OT (occupational therapist) and worked on things that his speech therapist told him to do. His mind is

SHARP. His body, not as much. His sense of humor and his smile have re-emerged though, making us all laugh. With his raspy voice, he has been able to say a few words but gets very frustrated when he can't get out what is in his head. The same goes for his hands and feet. Although he still has a way to go, the doctors and nurses are shocked by how far he has come. His nurses who were with him last week and just returned to work could not believe he is the same patient.

Kevin has been good with responding when we tell him we love him. He will give us a thumbs up or try and sign I love you but I got the sweetest gift today from him. He motioned me over. Usually, when I get close enough, he ends up coughing in my face (only a mother could love that) so I braced myself. Instead, with all he had, he slowly raised his arms some to put around me for a hug. That was it, best gift ever.

From Merrill Domas, Mame's college classmate and friend:
Chuck and Mary Ann,

I was shocked and so concerned to receive your email about Kevin. How worried you must be. I promise you I will be thinking and praying for him and for your whole family. Please keep me in the loop as he recovers.

Strangely enough, my daughter contracted a viral encephalitis while traveling in South East Asia. It took a year out of her life but, as bad as it was, it never reached the level of Kevin's.

I love you both and am so sorry that you are having to go through this.
With love and prayers.

March 8<u>th</u>

From Chuck/Dad/Poppa/Uncle Chunk:

I inadvertently omitted a very important part of today's news. Kevin will be moving from the neurological ICU to step-down as soon as a bed becomes available, likely today. This is a magnificent milestone.

Please continue to pray for Kevin and his family.
Love.

From Ed Matthews:
Wonderful: My day officially starts when I read the updates about Kevin. It appears that he has a good deal of his grandfather in him.
Semper Fi.

From Doyce Payne:
"To God be the Glory, great things He has done."

From Kay Payne:
WOW!! The Power of Prayer!! Praise God from whom all Blessings flow!!
Love.

From Dawn Chiaramonte Mansfield:
Kevin had his Quinton central line catheter removed from his neck today. We are one step closer to being "wireless." PT came in at 4 today to work with Kevin but he was too tired to do much. He spent most of the day sleeping or coughing. Let's hope that doesn't mean he will be up all night. He did manage to write Jeter's name (his dog) on his whiteboard. He wanted to know how he was.

[Chas and I grabbed a quick lunch in the cafeteria today. We were gone from Kevin's room for about 40 minutes or so (the longest he has been left alone since being in the hospital). When we returned, Kevin was frustrated, so with help from us trying to decode his writing and what his raspy voice was saying, we got "I've been calling you for an hour." Gotta love this boy!]

From Ann Donahue, wife of J. Christopher Donahue, President and CEO of Federated Hermes, Inc.:
Chuck - Chris and I are blasting the heavens for Kevin. I feel confident that God has Kevin on His radar. Thank you for keeping us on the updates. Chris is off to a silent retreat this weekend so be assured of a surge of prayers.
God's Grace Abound!

From Peter Meaney, Chuck's cousin:

I hope you are doing OK. I've been seeing updates on Kevin's progress on Facebook and it looks like he's slowly getting better. My prayers and thoughts are with you and the family every day. ... Give Dawn and Chas a hug for me and tell them I'm thinking of them. I'm sure your Mom is doing what she can to help Kevin through this. She was a Guardian Angel on earth for me, so I'm sure she is a Guardian Angel for her Great Grandson and she will help get him through this.

All the best to you and Mary Ann.

March 9th

From Dawn Chiaramonte Mansfield:

Exactly two weeks (almost to the minute) in Neuro ICU and WE HAVE FINALLY BEEN TRANSFERRED! We are now in the Neuro Step-Down Unit - 6F Room 6815.

Kevin's day started with PT where they had him on a slanted bed. They stood him up to put some pressure on his feet. He did well for his first time. He is holding his head up a little more each day. Next Kevin's speech therapist worked with him on swallowing. His feeding tube cannot be removed until he can swallow on a regular basis without coughing/gagging. Then he spent a few hours sitting in the recliner, a place he seems to find comfortable.

Aside from a couple of nosebleeds and then having to change the tape on his feeding tube, I would say we have settled nicely into our new room.

Keep those prayers coming. I truly believe Kevin is where he is now because of all his prayer warriors.

March 10th

From Linda Giarraputo Jeans:

Chuck, thanks so much for including me on the updates for Kevin. I have forwarded them to my prayer circle, forever to be known as "Prayer Warriors."

I assume Kevin is a senior. I know he is blessed with loving grandparents and now it is obvious he is blessed with strong parents. Prayers of healing for this young man.

God's blessings.

From Frank Cutney, Chuck's Chaminade classmate and friend of nearly 62 years:
Keep the good news coming! There is an angel on his shoulder and with his Mom!

From Dawn Chiaramonte Mansfield:

Today was a low-key day. Kevin worked with PT. He had a few visitors but, most importantly, he spent quality time with just his siblings. It was a joy to watch and listen to them smiling/laughing and a reminder to us all just how important family is.

I think today was an adjustment day for me concerning Kevin's care. Kevin was fortunate to have excellent care and amazing nurses in ICU. There was one nurse to two patients and Kevin was watched constantly. You could leave the room and know that he was safe. Things are different in this unit. Ratio is 1-6 and they check on patients every two hours unless an alarm goes off or you call them. Although the staff is nice and they do their job, there is no way I feel comfortable leaving Kevin alone. It's an unsettling feeling. An example: last night Kevin and I fell asleep. I woke up 30 minutes later to Kevin frantically coughing. His nose had started bleeding and his face and hand were covered in blood. (FYI: nothing serious just irritated by his feeding tube.) It made me wonder what would have happened if I weren't there. How long before someone got to him? No alarm went off and he couldn't call for anyone. Lesson learned.

March 11th

From Dawn Chiaramonte Mansfield:
Kevin's day of rest, although they did come in and get him to do some PT. He woke up showing off to me. He was opening and closing his fingers

all by himself and pulled his head up off the bed. He was so proud of himself. He gave a fist pump. The doctors have said they want him to get to rehab to start intensive work asap so after his next session with the speech therapist they will make a decision if he is ready to have the feeding tube removed from his nose because he can swallow correctly or if he needs to have a peg line, which is have the tube temporarily in his stomach. Either way I know Kevin will be happy to have that out of his nose.

From Mary Ann and Chuck Mansfield:

Joe Altman was our brother-in-law and one of God's greatest. When he died suddenly ten years ago, his loss was devastating to legions of friends and family. But our loss was heaven's gain, for Joe is truly an angel.

On March 19 Joe would have been 75. At the suggestion of his widow, we ask that each of you offer a kind deed for Kevin's recovery on that day. It could be a prayer, a smile to a stranger, a reach-out to a lonely friend, carrying a package for a neighbor, any act dedicated as a prayer for Kevin's recovery.

Thank you to all for the prayers and loving support shown to Kevin and his family. We will continue to send updates on his recovery which, with your help, will be sooner rather than later.

Gratefully.

March 12th

From Terry and Craig Middleton, lifelong friends:
Glad to hear about continued progress. Kevin is a real fighter.

March 13th

From Mary Ann Mansfield:
Hi, Maureen (Lally-Green),
Here's the latest about Kevin. As you know, Kevin, age 18, suffered a coma due to Acute Necrotizing Encephalopathy Myelitis (ANEM). He has emerged from the coma, and he no longer requires any respiratory

assistance, thankfully! He had his feeding tube removed and replaced with a PEG tube in his abdomen. The staff has recommended that he start rehabilitation as soon as possible, and their strong first suggestion was the Levine Pediatric Rehabilitation at Levine Children's Hospital in the Carolina's Healthcare System. Did you tell me that you had a cousin who is instrumental at Carolina's Healthcare? If so, could you refer us to him so Kevin might be admitted? We have been informed there is a long waiting list. (Authors' note: Maureen Lally-Green is a retired Pennsylvania judge and Chuck's fellow board member at Federated Hermes, Inc.)

March 14<u>th</u>

Journal entry from Dawn Chiaramonte Mansfield:
Kevin started the day off a little sluggish (a drawback from yesterday's meds). PT came to work with him but he didn't have the energy he usually has. He has gotten the all clear from his doctors to be released and head over to rehabilitation. We are just waiting on the specifics. Kevin slept a lot more this afternoon but when he woke up he was coughing less and trying to speak more. He is very proud of his accomplishments as are we.
(Kevin wanted to know when he was going to rehab and when he could start training. I asked him what he thought he needed to work on the most when he got there? His response: Speed. I love my boy!)

From Deborah and Jake Kleinschuster, friends; Jake is Chuck's Basic School classmate, fellow Marine and Vietnam War veteran:
YES, I will pray for the complete return of all Kevin's brain functions. My insides are still shaking at all your family has and is going through. God is capable of a complete healing and that is the way I will be praying. Please keep me posted on specific prayer needs as they arise in this healing process. I will address each need in prayer. You may text the need to my phone; it is always with me.
Sending Unending Prayers.
Love.

March 15th

From Donna and John Webster:
Thanks Chuck, appreciate the updates. Grateful that Kevin continues to make progress. What an amazing support team he has and God is on his side. We will keep the prayers going for him and all the Mansfield clan. Love.

From Denny Golden, Chuck's friend, fellow Holy Cross alumnus, fellow Marine and President Emeritus of Fontbonne University, St. Louis, MO:
Kevin's courage and determination are outstanding!
He is leading all of us.

From Kay Payne:
Chuck,
I love Kevin's response! Speed!! That alone is a good sign of cognitive ability. Praise God! Prayers continuing for Kevin and your loved ones!

From Mary Ann Mansfield:
Here is the grandmother's update:
Seeing Kevin after his release from ICU two weeks after a devastating diagnosis in a critical but stable condition was one of the hardest things I've ever done. I saw my beautiful full-of-life grandson struggling to talk, unable to walk or focus his eyes, and aware of everything going on around him. He managed a smile when he heard me and his helplessness nearly broke my heart. His parents assured me Kev was "miles" from when he was first admitted, one baby step at a time, but all I could see were the miles yet to go and no way to know how far he would go.

I've been here two days now and I'm beginning to see the baby steps. His family remains so optimistic and the attitude is catching. He is moving to a rehab facility today, even though he still has a peg line for feeding and can't walk on his own. The neurologist is shocked at his progress but knows the most effective therapies have to be administered within the first few months after brain trauma.

I know that faith and prayers will propel Kevin to wellness. Please continue to storm heaven for him! Gratefully.

From Lori Hensler:
Hi Chuck and Mame –
I saw the update from Dee (Marley, Federated Hermes, Inc.) today and I'm so relieved to hear of Kevin's progress. This is fantastic news! God is good.
Still praying for him though! This must be incredibly stressful for you both. Please take good care and we'll keep all of you in our thoughts and prayers.

March 16<u>th</u>

From Merrill Domas:
Sounds like a strong determined young man. Keeping him in my prayers.

From Terry and Craig Middleton:
Faith in God, belief in Kevin and trust in the doctors will turn the baby steps into miles. Kevin can draw strength from his family and from the prayers of his friends. We will both continue to pray. Love.

From Dawn Chiaramonte Mansfield:
First full day of therapy. 7am and Kevin was off and running...(ok, maybe not running!). He got to take his first shower and all he could say at the time was that it was the weirdest thing he ever felt. His OT worked with him on getting dressed and ready for the day. Next came speech. His therapist tried to get him to drink some juice to see how his swallowing was progressing. For those who don't know Kevin's likes/dislikes, juice isn't happening. So instead, he swallowed a thickened liquid to see how he was doing. One thing Kevin has to work on is getting the saliva to the back of his mouth and swallow. They decided to do a swallow study on Wednesday to check the vocal cords and make sure there is no damage to them. PT came next and Kevin worked for

90 minutes in the gym. We ended the day back in the gym with OT again. This time he got to do something he isn't allowed to do at home: play ball in the house. He was happy to (try and) throw the ball back and forth. He had a couple of visitors and then he was asleep by 9:30 ready to do it all again tomorrow...NOT!

(Kevin: called someone an idiot.

Mom: Kevin, that is not nice.

Kevin: Yes it was, that was pig Latin.)

Kevin at home with his Dad and giving another two thumbs up.
(Photograph courtesy of Dawn Mansfield and published with her permission.)

March 22nd

From Mary Ann Mansfield:

Just returned from an emotionally and physically challenging week in Charlotte. First, seeing Kevin in such a diminished state was shocking despite assurances that he had improved with each passing day. I stayed with my sister Bernice (who lives in Charlotte) and she admitted that when she first saw Kevin in the early days, she was praying that his parents would not have to make the decision to leave his respirator on for the rest of his life, or turn it off. Chas and Dawn remain positive and anticipate a recovery baby-step by step. When the road is long, I pray the steps continue forward.

I was heartened by the progress I saw while I was there. The therapists (occupational, physical, speech, cognitive and psychological) and the doctors who specialize in brain injury are wonderful. Kevin's brain is sharp and I think that might fuel his fears about his limitations and the tasks ahead.

Chuck and I are driving up to Charlotte on March 28th and returning April 3rd. Haven't made definite plans to return to NY and the weather is off-putting!

I know Dawn plans to write thank you notes when she has a minute, but we wanted to thank you personally for your generous financial support and ongoing prayerful one.

Love to you all and Happy Easter.

From Joanne and Roger Hunt:

We were so happy to hear you feel encouraged after your visit with Kevin and are impressed with his doctors and staff. Undoubtedly, when you return for Easter, you will notice much more progress. Hopefully, the fact that his mind is sharp will be a motivation for him to work hard with his therapists towards a full recovery.

We don't blame you for delaying choosing a date to return to Westhampton. All our friends back home are so fed up with the never ending Northeasters and losing power with each storm. They are all suffering from cabin fever.

Vanessa and all the family are driving here this weekend for the kids' spring break and will stay a week. We are all so excited.

Yesterday was Taylor's follow up appointment to her recent MRI with her neurologist and oncologist. They said she is looking great and doesn't have to have another MRI for six months !!!! (She has been having an MRI every three months for the past three years.) Obviously, we are all thrilled!

We hope you have a wonderful Easter, celebrating many more baby steps for Kevin.

Love and prayers for you all.

From Merrill Domas:

Mary Ann, you guys have really been on my mind. I can only imagine how hard this has been.

We all have such special love for our grandchildren and strive to protect them in every way. Seeing one go through this must be incredibly painful for all of you. It is heartening to hear about his progress and I hope and pray it will continue. I am sending my love and prayers along to you. You will remain in my thoughts. Love.

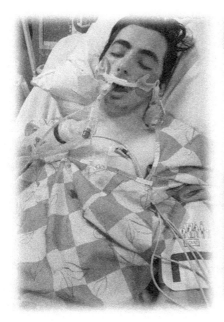 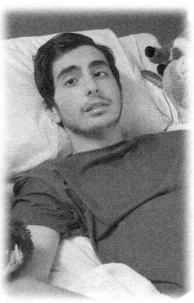

Kevin comatose…and three weeks later.
(Photographs courtesy of Dawn Mansfield and published with her permission.)

MY FIRST HOSPITAL VISIT WITH KEVIN

By Chuck Mansfield

*You know, life fractures us all into little pieces. It harms us,
but it's how we glue those fractures back together that makes us stronger.*

– Carrie Jones

On March 28, 2018, Mame and I drove from Hutchinson Island to Charlotte to visit with Kevin and his family, and to celebrate his father's 50th birthday on April 2nd. It would be my first visit with them since Kevin became ill just over a month before. Based on Mame's initially dreadful account of Kevin's physical condition, I believe it's fair to say that I was prepared for the worst. What I encountered is clearly portrayed in my tube-ridden and ostensibly inert grandson's image as depicted in the photograph of "Kevin comatose" on the preceding page. As they say, a picture is worth a thousand words.

By way of background, Kevin and I have always enjoyed an honest, high-spirited, loving and jocular relationship, which morphed into "zinging" each other in his pre-teen years. Now my dictionary tells me that to "zing" is "to move swiftly, particularly if making a high-pitched buzzing sound, or to criticize someone." Well, I don't know about moving "swiftly" or the "high-pitched buzzing sound" but playful criticism is my focus here. To be sure, this was largely good-natured stuff but, too often to Mame's chagrin, our zingers were occasionally laced with profanity, but I digress. To provide the reader an innocuous example, Kevin might address me and say, "Poppa, you really are old and ugly." My rejoinder might be, "Shut up and drop dead, you little twit." Anyway, you get the idea.

Upon entering Kevin's hospital room, I thought he was asleep, possibly still unconscious. What happened was uplifting and hilarious. As I greeted those in the room – and there were several family members and friends on hand – Kevin opened his eyes, attempted to sit up and, tubes notwithstanding, in a loud voice, asked, "Hi, Poppa, how are you, you old fart!?" In that memorable moment I knew that my grandson's mind, sense of humor and "zinging" capacities were still fully intact. As Judy Garland sang in 1938, "Zing! Went the strings of my heart." Indeed, Kevin's performance brought the house down and me laughter and great joy. YES!

A young priest administers the Sacrament of
the Anointing of the Sick to Kevin.
*(Photograph courtesy of Dawn Mansfield and
published with her permission.)*

KEVIN SEAN MANSFIELD, R.O.A.

By Chuck Mansfield

The initials R.O.A. stand for Rinkachous of America, a secret organization founded in 1957 by Kevin's great uncle, Michael Mansfield, my highly creative brother, then ten years old. In this connection, for the sake of authenticity, Mike actually produced with colored pencils handwritten certificates of membership for each of the R.O.A.'s then three (!) members: Denis Murphy, Mike and yours truly. (Murph's is still extant, framed and on display in my Florida home.) Each certificate was duly signed by "Draw-Boink-Boink, General President." The Rinkachous also had the equivalent of a secret handshake, a "salute" that required the quick, awkward and somewhat difficult flashing of one's left hand under one's raised right knee, a serious greeting that stands to this day and is increasingly challenging for the aging. Also thanks to its founder, the fledgling R.O.A. had its own anthem, which the original members still sing by tradition and from memory on solemn and, sometimes, not-so-solemn occasions. Here it is:

RINKACHOUS OF AMERICA!
RINKACHOUS FOREVER!
WE WILL FIGHT, WE WILL FIGHT
UNTIL THE WAR IS OVER
AND WE'LL WIN, WE'LL WIN
AGAINST THE BEEKEECHOUS!
WE WILL RAISE OUR FLAG UP HIGH IN THE SKY
IT WILL WAVE THROUGH THE AIR
AND DRAW-BOINK-BOINK WILL BE THERE!
JAR SAW WILL BE SINGING
AND THE BELLS, THEY WILL BE RINGING!
HINKLE HINEYBONE WILL STAND

LEADING HIS MUSICAL BAND!
CHUCK AND MURPH WILL SALUTE
AND MIKE WILL PLAY THE FLUTE!

Readers may wonder about the names heralded in the anthem. Understand first that the R.O.A. was and remains, for better or worse, an all-male society. The "Beekeechous," the Rinkachous' principal adversaries and rival organization, were all-female, composed primarily of Mike's and my then-three sisters. (Our youngest sister, Mary Kay or Kate, as she is now known, had not yet been born!) "Jar Saw," a Norwegian by birth, Mike once informed me, is a senior official of the R.O.A., as is "Hinkle Hineybone."

"And now," as the late great radio commentator Paul Harvey used to say, "for the rest of the story."

Enter Kevin Sean Mansfield, age thirteen. Somehow he had learned, perhaps via his father, of this mysterious secret organization called the Rinkachous of America. Almost immediately he began a lobbying campaign that would last some four years. Courageous, irrepressible, perseverant and undaunted, Kevin forcefully and repeatedly made his key point that the R.O.A. needed new blood. After all, he reminded us that the old guard, if you will, had been around for more than fifty years, and the original Rinkachous were now in their sixties. Founding R.O.A. member Uncle Mike took Kevin's ardently proposed membership under advisement with the Rinkachou immortals: Draw-Boink-Boink, Jar Saw and Hinkle Hineybone. Alas, from Kevin's perspective, their rendered decision was negative.

Disappointed but not dissuaded, Kevin bounced back and redoubled his efforts with extraordinary grit and determination. Indeed, my grandson seemed to view his R.O.A. membership as a rite of passage and clearly would let nothing stand in his way. The fact that no one from his father's generation, not even his father, had ever been granted membership in the R.O.A. over its many decades was inconsequential to him. In my opinion, that omission or oversight – call it what you will – became in Kevin's view a critical reason why *his* membership mattered all the more.

Still, another year passed and another negative verdict came from the R.O.A.'s elders.

Then, at a dinner celebration of Kevin's grandfather's 70th birthday on April 10, 2015, Rinkachous founder Uncle Mike, with fellow Rinkachou Denis Murphy in attendance, announced that his great-nephew Kevin Sean Mansfield – and great he is! – had at last been granted membership in the Rinkachous of America. It was a joyous day for all but for Kevin especially it was the culmination of tenacity, hard work and never taking no for an answer when the stakes were high and the outcome mattered dearly. Way to go, Kevin!

RINKACHOUS FOREVER!

Kevin, age 18, sporting New York Mets colors (orange jacket and suspenders with blue shirt and trousers) on June 17, 2017, at the Westhampton Country Club in New York although he was a staunch Yankees fan at the time.
(Photograph courtesy of Elizabeth Boyce and published with her permission.)

KEVIN AND GENESIUS

By Chuck Mansfield

As recorded often and elsewhere, Kevin has been an accomplished actor. Indeed, his credits are acclaimed in writing by both his father and grandmother earlier in this work.

Based on research during a visit to www.earlychurchhistory.org, I paraphrase and provide here biographical information on the courageous Genesius and later report on how Kevin connected with this early Christian.

The ancient Roman actor Genesius was a leader/member of a troupe of actors who performed comedic plays regularly for Emperor Diocletian, who reigned from 284 to 305.

At the time, actors specialized in satire on many subjects, and Genesius was a favorite of the Emperor. One evening the play's focus was to ridicule the burgeoning sect of Christians, whom Diocletian hated, persecuted and killed. Genesius' role was to pretend to be baptized.

Genesius obviously had attended several Christian baptisms in order to be familiar with his role. He was supposed to be sick and fell to the floor. The appointed "priest" and "exorcist" rushed onto the stage. Genesius said he was burdened by his sins and an angel had commanded him to be baptized to wipe them all away. Everyone was laughing uncontrollably. Genesius insisted he wanted to be baptized and the priest poured water on him but then he stood up and told the audience of Diocletian, his court and all the other actors that he was serious. He had just become a Christian and could still see the angel who spoke to him. The priest threw a white robe over him in imitation of a catechumen, a Christian convert under instruction before baptism.

Genesius would not play the part. Instead, he addressed the Emperor and all those around him and exhorted them to give their lives to Christ. So serious and persistent was he that the Emperor became enraged and had Genesius turned over to the prefect of the Praetorian Guard to be tortured.

Under torture, Genesius still insisted that he had been converted right there and then onstage and would not renounce Christ. Seeing it was a true conversion to Christianity, Diocletian had him beheaded in the early 300s. Genesius played the part of a new Christian, became the part, and was tortured and decapitated because he actually became what he portrayed.

Hearing the news of his death, Christians realized that Genesius had indeed been converted and martyred for his faith. They secured his body and buried him in the Cemetery of St. Hippolytus on the Via Tiburtina. (Hippolytus had been torn to pieces limb by limb fifty years earlier.)

As logic would suggest, Genesius became the patron of actors, dancers, musicians, comedians and converts. But he is also the patron saint of thieves, epileptics, printers, torture victims and lawyers. Go figure.

A Roman Catholic organization, founded by Pope John II and Pope Benedict XVI called The Fraternity of St. Genesius, has as its purpose to encourage Catholics to participate in the renewal of culture as part of the New Evangelization. Members pray for those involved in theatrical and cinematic arts, and St. Genesius is their patron. I understand that the new Fraternity has been especially well received in Ireland.

To be sure, Kevin has always been entertaining. In her poem earlier herein, his Aunt Katie describes him variously as "sensitive," "playful" and "humorous." She is right, and you will recall his "zinging" prowess. Never shy, he is a born performer. Not surprisingly he discovered in early high school that he loved drama, musicals and acting. Indeed, he is a natural.

In May 2015, Mame and I flew to Charlotte to surprise Marissa and Kevin, who both had major roles in Charlotte Catholic High School's production of Disney's *Beauty and the Beast*. Marissa starred in the title role as Belle, and Kevin played LeFou, a role that was made for him or vice versa. (LeFou is from the French *le fou*, which means the fool, who is Gaston's snide, accident-prone sidekick.) Both grandchildren's performances were, in a word, brilliant.

The following year, both Marissa and Kevin had roles in Charlotte Catholic's spring musical *Shrek* in which Kevin gave another hilarious and outstanding performance as a donkey. In the role Kevin cleverly affected an accent that combined the vocal sounds of a gay man and those of an African-American man. His performance was so hilarious that the man seated behind me told his companion that he had already seen the show on the prior evening but returned because he wanted to see a repeat by Kevin. "That kid is a riot!" he exclaimed.

Today, as in days of yore, young Catholic *confirmandi* choose a saint's name to take as their Confirmation name. Kevin, who enjoys both providing and receiving surprises, surprised his family and friends by choosing the name – you guessed it – Genesius for his Confirmation. Truth be told, none of us had ever heard of Saint Genesius and some of us even wondered at first if Kevin might have made up the name. After all, his imagination is beyond vivid. In the final analysis, he deserves great credit, for he did his research and made his decision. Kevin was confirmed in 2015.

God bless you, Kevin Sean Genesius Mansfield!

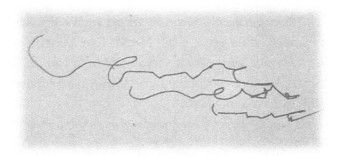

Kevin's first attempt at writing, post-coma.
Who knew we had a Sanskrit scholar in the family?
*(Photograph courtesy of Dawn Mansfield and
published with her permission.)*

A TRAGIC ACCIDENT AT AGE 18 AND A GREAT LIFE THEREAFTER

By Jack Stillwaggon

I do believe that when we face challenges in life that are far beyond our own power, it's an opportunity to build on our faith, inner strength, and courage. I've learned that how we face challenges plays a big role in the outcome of them.

– Sasha Azavedo

Jack is a friend, a fellow Chaminade High School alumnus, a fellow Marine and a Vietnam-era veteran. Chuck and he served together for several years as board members of the Marine Corps Scholarship Foundation Long Island chapter. During his career, Jack served as a senior executive in both product and service companies in the U.S., Latin America, Europe and Asia.

His essay "Thoughts on the Vietnam War: Did We Win or Lose?" was published in Chuck's third book, VIETNAM: Remembrances of a War, in June 2018. The following article is excerpted from Chuck's 2019 book, LEADERSHIP: In Action, Thought and Word, where it was published under the title "A Leadership Style."

In this essay Jack writes admirably and warmly of his father, Captain Jim Stillwaggon, whose foot was crushed in a tugboat accident and subsequently amputated at age 18, and who went on to manage a highly successful career and lead an exemplary and fulfilling life.

Jack and his wife Barbara live in Connecticut.

Kindness, decency and a genuine regard for others as a foundation.

KEVIN COURAGEOUS

Imagine a teenager growing up during the depression on an island town within the city limits of New York. You dream of someday becoming a Naval Aviator like those heroes you've seen in the exciting movies. A biplane comes to town selling rides for $5 and you offer to wax the plane every day that week for a free ride. The flyer departs a day earlier than scheduled and you never get that ride.

You win a diving and swimming scholarship to college but your parents forbid it because it's a Protestant school and you're a Catholic. Instead, you go to work on the tugboats like your father and grandfather did before you. At 18 years old, your foot is crushed between the tugboat and a barge. The foot is amputated and you receive a payment of only $300 from the tugboat company to compensate you for your loss.

Many people would be depressed or at least discouraged. They would assume the role of the victim and seek a handout. Lost career opportunities, a missed chance to be the first in your family to get a higher education and worst of all a debilitating permanent injury. No, not for you. Months of operations and rehabilitation at the Merchant Marine hospital pass and you return to work. First, you're a cook and then a deckhand. After studying and passing Coast Guard exams, you become a First Mate and then a Captain. All you want is to marry your childhood sweetheart and do the best job you can.

That young man became my father. Everyone has always commented on his sunny disposition and positive spirit. Yet, you can't just be a nice guy and also lead tough men like tugboat crews. Captain Jim gave the men some slack at times but the deal was that the job must get done. The men went out of their way to keep the union from routinely reassigning them to another boat. Some even gave up time off to avoid it.

My father ran on the reform ticket of the union trying to get more time off for the members. When a tugboat man is working he's on the boat 24/7. He tried to get two weeks on and two weeks off instead of just one week off. Due to collusion between the union bosses and the tugboat companies, his effort was voted down and the men received a 25-cents-an-hour raise, which cost the companies far less money.

My father got a break when he was able to collect on an old favor his father had done for the owner of a harbor pilot firm based in the New York City area. He studied day and night for the various licenses having to recreate charts from memory and assisting on ships without pay as a form of apprenticeship. Eventually, he was voted president of that company, Interport Pilots. They did business in New England and New York mostly but my father worked in the UK, the Emirates, the Caribbean and other exotic places. He was chosen to pilot the Queen's yacht when she and Prince Philip visited the US. He piloted VLCCs [Very Large Crude Carriers], the largest of the fuel tankers, much bigger than the super tankers. He used to like to say they are as big as the Empire State building on its side.

Let me explain what a harbor pilot does. When a ship arrives near a port, the captain has no knowledge of the depths, currents and peculiarities of the port. He requires the help of a local harbor pilot to guide the ship safely into the harbor and to the dock, which requires great skill. To get out to sea to meet the ship, the pilot rides from the harbor on a pilot boat, say, a fifty-foot boat with a cabin and hand rails to hold onto while grabbing the Jacob's ladder on the ship to climb up to the deck. You might be picturing this occurring on a calm, sunny day with no waves. Another possibility is five foot swells in the pitch black of a winter night with ice formed on the ladder. The pilot boat operator has to approach the ship which is either at anchor or just barely moving forward. He needs to get the boat close enough to the ship to give the pilot as much help as possible to successfully complete this dangerous task. At the same time, he needs to avoid damaging the boat and the ship. If the pilot falls into the sea, which happened to my father in his late sixties, in winter and at night, the pilot boat operator has to avoid crushing the pilot between the two vessels and then find a way to haul him back on deck. I wanted to make this clear because it is the basis for an anecdote about Captain Jim's leadership style.

I attended a lecture on boating safety at my yacht club. The instructor saw my nametag and came over to shake my hand and ask if I were related to a Captain Jim Stillwaggon. I told him that he was my father. He got a big smile and said, "What a great man!" He told me the following story of how he met my father and the lasting impression it made on him.

"When I was hired as an operator of a 50-foot boat by Interport Pilots, I was told to meet them on board at Goat Island in Newport, Rhode Island. I showed up, a little nervous at meeting the pilots. None of them spoke to me more than to say that the boss would be there soon and just to wait. They chatted with each other and I just cooled my heels. Then, your father arrived and brushed right past his partners and made a beeline for me. He gave me a big smile and a hearty handshake and welcomed me to Interport. Then, he got the attention of his partners and said, 'Gentlemen, this is the most important man on the boat! Our lives are in his hands.' Wow, did that make me feel great! I went from being invisible a minute ago to MVP."

I thanked him for telling me about the incident. I never would have known. It made me reflect on the many times that people spoke so highly of him.

KEVIN'S GIGGLES

By Kevin Sean and Dawn Chiaramonte Mansfield

Dawn, Kevin's Mom, introduces this chapter accordingly: "These are conversations, comments, blurbs straight from Kevin's mouth. This showed us just how the brain really does have a mind of its own. What made us giggle at these is that they were exactly what Kevin was thinking. He wasn't trying to make us laugh; we just laughed in spite of it. Enjoy!"

Of "Giggles" Chuck's lifelong friend, Chaminade and Holy Cross classmate and teammate Tom Kiley has written, "Poignant humor is in a very different category than mere jokes. Not much else to say therefore except that you never cut funny. These [are] instinctive and unvarnished comedic moments between a loving mother and her wounded but still witty son."

Here we go.

While *Kevin was sleeping soundly in ICU, Chas and I grabbed a quick lunch in the cafeteria. We were gone from Kevin's room for about 30 minutes (the longest he had been left without a parent since being admitted). When we returned, Kevin was awake and frustrated, so with help from us trying to decode his writing and what his raspy voice was trying to say, we got:*
Kevin: I've been calling you for well over an hour. Where is your phone?

After finally figuring out what Kevin was trying to spell out, we got it. He was writing his dog's name, Jeter.
Kevin: Justin sucks.
Mom: Why would you say that?
Turns out he thought Justin wasn't caring for the dog and hadn't fed him all this time.

Kevin wanted to know when he was going to rehab and when he could start training.

Mom: What do you need to work on most when we get there? (*Speech, physical therapy, occupational therapy, etc.*)
Kevin: Speed, running a 4.4 40-yard dash and being able to dunk.

Dad: Kevin, you may not realize it, but God hand-picked you to carry a message for everyone from Him about hope and faith.
Expecting something heartfelt, and without a beat, he got:
Kevin: Don't fart with your pants down!

Kevin: Marissa, I'm going on strike with the oil workers.

These three conversations were all within minutes of each other.
Doctor: Kevin, do you know why you are in the hospital?
Kevin: Yes, I sprained my ankle.
Nurse: Kevin, do you know why you are here?
Kevin: Yes, I had a stroke.
Certified Nursing Assistant: Kevin, do you know why you are here?
Kevin: Yes, I have cancer.
He was very surprised every time we told him 'No.' He was just as surprised when we told him he had the flu.

I need to set the scene for this. The room is dark, and Kevin is asleep. I finally settle in the broken recliner and am just starting to doze when Kevin SCREAMS for me. I jump up, trying to put the recliner down. It doesn't go down. Kevin is still screaming so I try to jump out of it but instead, I flip out of it onto Kevin's bed with the chair following me. Flustered, concerned and in a bit of pain now...
Kevin: MOM!!!!!
Mom: What's wrong, Kev?!
Kevin: I didn't fall.
Mom: That's great honey. Why are you telling me this?
Kevin: I called you.
Mom: I know but why? (*Still tangled in the chair*)
Kevin: They told me don't fall.
Mom: Who told you?

Kevin: The people upstairs. (*Kevin points towards upstairs and proceeds to go right back to sleep*).
There is a sign on the ceiling of the room to remind patients to stay in bed. It says, "Call Don't Fall!"
At this time, I am completely on the floor, laughing under the chair, and all I can think of is, I need the call button so I can say "Help, I've Fallen, and I Can't Get Up!"

Kevin: I met a mermaid
Mom: Oh really? Where?
Kevin: On the beach.
Mom: Did you say anything?
Kevin: She said hi.
Mom: What did she look like?
Kevin: Oh God, she was ugly!

Later...
Kevin: Screw Hawaii!
Mom: What do you mean? Why?
Kevin: I went to Hawaii, Mom.
Mom: When?
Kevin: The other day.
Mom: Was that when you met the mermaid?
Kevin: Yes.
Mom: Is that why you went to Hawaii?
Kevin: You don't go to Hawaii for mermaids, Mom, you go to surf!

Doctor: Kevin, do you know where you are?
Kevin: Yes, Canada,
Doctor: You are not in Canada.
Kevin: I'm not? (*Shocked face*)

Nurse: Do you know where you are, Kevin?
Kevin: Toronto.
Nurse: No, not Toronto.

KEVIN COURAGEOUS

Kevin: Buffalo.
Nurse: You are in Charlotte.
Kevin: I am? That's where I live!

Kevin's feeding tube alarm will beep when the bag is almost empty. Kevin hates any of the beeping sounds (Sensory issues). The alarm starts to beep.
Kevin: Don't worry, Mom. I'm not dead. The alarm didn't flat line.

After cleaning something off Kevin's tooth.
Mom: All done.
Kevin: Oh good, I could have died.
Mom: You are not going to die from me cleaning your tooth.
Kevin: Are you, really, sure of that?

Marissa: What are you looking at?
Kevin: The chicken.
Marissa: What chicken?
Kevin: On your head...bock, bock.

Kevin: I beat cancer and Brooke is coming. Best day ever!

Before his illness, Kevin would tell us that Helen Keller didn't really exist. He was relentless. Somehow, her name came up in conversation.
Mom: Helen Keller was real.
Kevin: Yes, she was. She hung herself in a tree, but nobody knew because they couldn't hear her.

Kevin: Mom, I need help.
Mom: What do you need, Kev?
Kevin: I need you to move the month of July.
Mom: What?
Kevin: It needs to go after December.
Mom: You can't move months around.
Kevin: Mom, you're a Mom. Moms can move things.

Kevin played Donkey in his high school musical, Shrek. His friend brought him a stuffed donkey which stayed with Kevin his whole journey.
Kevin: Mom, I was just talking to Donkey.
Mom: What did you say?
Kevin: I told him he was an ass.

Another quiet night and Kevin, in a panic, yells to me:
Kevin: Mom, I can't breathe (*as he is holding his breath*).
Mom: Open your mouth, Kev.
Kevin: Oh, that works.

Kevin: I need to find my sister. She is lost. She is at Aunt Bernice's house. Tell her to find her way here.

Kevin: We are in Canada.
Mom: We are not in Canada.
Kevin: It doesn't matter, I'm going to Arizona.
Mom: How are you getting to Arizona?
Kevin: (*Exasperated*) On my plane.
Mom: What plane? Where did you get a plane?
Kevin: Mom, I'm a pilot. We all have planes.

Kevin: I beat cancer.
Mom: You didn't have cancer.
Kevin: I'm such a pansy.

Nurse: (*To me, while changing Kevin*) Do you know what size condom catheter they use?
Kevin: EXTRA LARGE!

Kevin: I died and came back to life.
Dad: You didn't die, you were in a coma.
Kevin: Oh, potato, tomato.

Dad: Who came and visited you today?
Kevin: The doctor.

Dad: Oh, what did he say?
Kevin: Hi, Kevin.
Dad: OK, what else did he say?
Kevin: Bye, Kevin.

Kevin called someone an idiot.
Mom: Kevin, that was not nice.
Kevin: Yes, it was. That was Pig Latin.

Kevin: Mamie was horrible today.
Mom: Why do you say that?
Kevin: Because I died.
Mom: You didn't die.
Kevin: I didn't? I'm not de-ad. I'm not de-ad!

During a loud thunderstorm. Kevin is still convinced he is in Canada.
Kevin: Canadian thunderstorms are no joke!

While looking at himself in the mirror.
Mom: What are you doing?
Kevin: Ssh, I don't want myself to hear you.

Mom: Tomorrow is Rock Your Socks Day.
Kevin: So?
Mom: We have to wear our mismatched socks to honor Ben.
Kevin: I'm sorry, I can't participate.
Mom: And why not?
Kevin: Because I have cancer.
Mom: You don't have cancer. You can participate.
Kevin: No, I can't. I have Down Syndrome.

Kevin stood up at the table, to do some physical therapy work.
Kevin: I am the president of the United States. Step aside Obama. (FYI: Trump is President.)

Trying to repeat his diagnosis for us.

Kevin: ANEM (*acute necrotizing encephalopathy myelitis*)
Mom: Caused from what?
Kevin: The flu.
Mom: Which strain? (*looking for A or B*)
Kevin: Strain of the vocal cords.

Therapist: I like the Mets.
Kevin: Boo, they are bad.
Therapist: They are getting better.
Kevin: Really, how long was I in the coma?

Kevin: Mom, the wire fell out.
Mom: What wire?
Kevin: My braces.
Mom: You haven't had braces in years.
Kevin: Then what is this on my teeth?
Mom: There is nothing there. You do not have braces.
Kevin: YES, I DO!
Tim: Here, look. (*Showing him a mirror*)
Kevin: Oh look, I told you, I don't have braces.

Talking about Brooke and Blake coming to visit.
Kevin: Coming here today. The three Bs. Brooke S, Blake J and BM. Bullshit, Blowjob and Bowel Movement. The Trifecta!

Kevin: Mr. Maddox, I have a proposition for you.
Leland: What's that?
Kevin: You pay me.
Leland: For what?
Kevin: For nothing, but I'm thinking $20 an hour.

During Kevin's Vision Evaluation.
Kevin: We pay you to tell me that I'm right eye dominant?

Finishing dinner, Kevin takes his last bite of chicken.

Kevin: As we stand here today, with this last bite of chicken, we remember Jesus Christ at the last supper as he said, Our Father, who art in heaven...

Kevin had a hat hanging on a medicine pole.
Tim: Why did they move Kevin's hat?
Mom: They moved the pole out of the room.
Tim: Which pole?
Kevin: My stripper pole!

Mom: A lot has happened in the world in the last four weeks, Kevin.
Kevin: (*Looking around*) What has happened to you?
Tim: Who are you talking to?
Kevin: The earth.

Kevin: (*Very upset*) Please don't leave me.
Mom: You will be ok. Justin is here with you.
Kevin: Please wait 'til Kaitlyn (*his therapist*) gets here?
Mom: Why?
Kevin: I'm afraid I'll die if Justin doesn't know what to do.
Mom: Justin is just here to keep you company. The nurses are here to take care of you.
Kevin: Why didn't you just say that then? Goodbye!

Kevin: I slept at Aunt Pamie's old house last night.
Mom: Really? What were you doing there?
Kevin: I had no place to stay while you and Dad where training for the Olympics.
Mom: The Olympics?! What were we training for?
Kevin: Figure skating.

Kevin: How do you greet your Jewish friends?
Mom: No idea. How?
Kevin: Shalomie Homie.

Kevin: Life is like a box of chocolates. You win some. You lose some.

Doctor: I just stopped in to say hi. (*He asks Kevin a few questions.*)
Kevin: (*to doctor*) Wow, that was a lot more than just hi!

Kevin: There are two reasons why I can't marry my therapist. Number 1… She is 30. Number 2… (*He begins laughing uncontrollably.*) I said number two (*continues laughing*). Number two is not why I can't. (*Laughing so hard he can't even finish his thought.*)

Kevin: You can never replace the legend!
Mom: He is a mess.
Kevin: I'm a hot mess, emphasis on HOT!

First visit with the speech therapist.
Kevin: I hear changes in my voice. Is it puberty or irregularity?

One of Kevin's ICU nurses was always on duty (no pun intended) when Kevin was in the coma and needed to be changed. When visiting her…
Kevin: What's my favorite number?
Nurse: I don't know. What is it?
Kevin: Number two. Get it? (*Again, uncontrollable laughter.*)

Kevin: Dad, can you put the blanket on me?
Dad: You can do it. It is right next to you.
Kevin: Dad, you signed up for this when you put your pee pee in the hole.

Dad: Do you know what you need to do, Kevin?
Kevin: Yes, learn how to have sex with a girl.

Kevin: Life is like a box of chocolates. You never know when you are gonna fart.

Kevin: Sometimes, I think I am a baby because I have to relearn everything. Hey, Mom, SURPRISE! You are the proud Mom of a 19-year-old baby. I'm so cute.

Kevin and the doctor were discussing his double vision.
Mom: If Aunt Pamie and I were sitting next to each other, you would see four of us.
Kevin: You two don't look anything alike anymore.
Mom: Really, since when?
Kevin: Since I could tell you apart.

Another of those quiet moments trying to nap. Do you hear the scream coming?
Kevin: MOM! MOM!
Mom: What is it, Kev?
Kevin: Are you dead?
Mom: NO.
Kevin: Oh good, go back to sleep.

Marissa: Kevin, you look so much better without that mustache. You can see how straight your teeth look.
Kevin: Mustaches don't grow on teeth.

Kevin still only drinks from a straw for fear of aspirating.
Marissa: Kevin, one year until you can drink legally.
Kevin: Yep, I'll be the first guy to drink a shot through a straw.

CRISIS AND THE FIVE FS

By Chuck Mansfield

I first developed and incorporated into my life the Five Fs when I got fired at age 45, some thirty years ago. For me losing one's job was, until then, something that happened only to someone else. I share the Five Fs with others who may be in a similar situation or even worse. My theory is that, if one keeps the Five Fs in proper perspective each day, the manageability of a crisis will be facilitated.

Of course, getting fired now pales in comparison to what Kevin has endured.

The topic is crisis, the plural of which is crises. From the Greek κριση (*krise*), it is "an emotionally significant event or radical change of status in a person's life."

- Have you ever had a crisis in your life? If so, how would you describe it?

- What would you say was your most important personal quality that enabled you to come through the crisis?

- What lesson(s) did you learn?

- Depending on one's age, we have all had crises in our lives. For example, I once had a senior executive position at a large financial institution in New York City, and I was terminated, along with 5,000 other people in order to save $300 million in expenses. As a result, my family income decreased 75%. If that's not a crisis…

- I have over the years counseled many individuals who were in job-search mode. Many of them lost their jobs due to a poor economy and/or corporate expense cutbacks, often called "downsizing." To be sure, loss of a position can have a serious psychological effect on an individual.

- One of the pieces of advice I give concerns what I call the daily "F" check. To weather a crisis, be it a job loss or something else maybe worse, it helps a great deal if a person each day considers these five words that begin with the letter F.

- The five Fs are Faith, Family, Friends, Fitness and Fortitude. For me faith is a religious element; for others it may simply be faith in oneself or self-confidence. Family and friends are important human elements who can and will typically be helpful and supportive of us during a time of stress. Fitness is essential, for a healthy body usually helps us maintain a healthy mind and a positive disposition. And fortitude, the inner strength to keep going, is actually a derivative of the first four Fs.

- If one can draw on them for strength during a crisis, and keep them in balance, I believe he, she or they will weather the storm.

ALEX AND JEAN TREBEK RECEIVE FORDHAM FOUNDER'S AWARD

By Tom Stoelker

According to Mr. Stoelker at www.tomstoelker.com, "I spent fifteen years as a freelance set designer and stylist with my work appearing in the pages of Architectural Digest *and the windows of Harvey Nichols in London. Later, I went to school and shifted my focus to English literature and photography and graduated* Summa Cum Laude, *Phi Beta Kappa from Lehman College, receiving my master's at Columbia Journalism School as a Bollinger fellow. From there I went on to write features for the* The Philadelphia Inquirer, The Wall Street Journal, The Architect's Newspaper, Landscape Architecture Magazine, *and* Modern Magazine. *I am now senior staff writer at Fordham University and continue to freelance, writing about the urban landscape and photographing events around New York City. I love to kayak New York City's waterways and cycle over its bridges; I volunteer as a docent at the Morris Jumel Mansion; and tend to my garden in Queens."*

Jeopardy! *quiz show host Alex Trebek, despite living with stage-four pancreatic cancer, continues at this writing to host the program, and speaks eloquently of giving "encouragement to others who are suffering" and the "power of prayer."*

Godspeed, Alex Trebek.

The following excerpts from Mr. Stoelker's article were published in University News *on January 10, 2020.*

Photos by Kait McKay. With the lights of Los Angeles flickering as a backdrop, Fordham University bestowed the Fordham Founder's Award on Alex and Jean Trebek at a presidential reception at the Bel-Air Country Club on Jan. 7. It was the first time that the award, represented by the weighty statuette of Fordham founder Archbishop John Hughes, had ever been given outside of New York City, though the Founder's Dinner will still be held in New York on March 30 [, 2020].

The iconic game-show host, who is living with stage four pancreatic cancer, arrived at the event straight from the studio still in makeup from recording five episodes of *Jeopardy!*. He told the crowd that he was there to provide comic relief from the formalities. Pointing to the statue, he noted that at 20 pounds it was the heaviest award he has ever received.

"That's about a case of beer for those of you who keep track of statistics," he mused.

On a more serious note, he acknowledged that his consistent appearance on the game show, despite his illness, has been an encouragement to others who are suffering.

"It's humbling and it's gratifying; because of the program that I have hosted for 36 years I have managed to touch the lives of so many people," he said.

He recalled a recent Lakers game that he attended where the sports announcer Mike Breen, FCRH '83, leaned in to remind him that there were "a lot of people praying" for him.

"And if there's one thing I have discovered in the past year it is that power of prayer; I learned it from the Jesuits when I was a kid, l learned it from the Oblates of Mary Immaculate when I was in boarding school," he said with tears in his eyes.

The Trebeks would go on to send their two children to Jesuit schools. Their daughter, Emily, graduated from Loyola Marymount University in Los Angeles in 2015 and their son, Matthew, graduated from Fordham College at Rose Hill with a degree in philosophy in 2013. Today Matthew is a restaurateur in Harlem, an area of the city that the couple has grown very fond of. They established the Alex Trebek Endowed Scholarship, making gifts of $2 million to aid Fordham students from North Harlem and East Harlem.

"You think Alex Trebek is a good man; you don't know the half of it, he's better than you think," said Joseph M. McShane, S.J., president of Fordham. "He's a brilliant man who is the nation's school teacher, let's admit that. As the host of *Jeopardy!*, he is our school teacher and we look forward to going to school every evening."

Father McShane called Trebek a man of "quiet generosity" who, even in tough times, continues to teach.

"He teaches us about how to live each day with purpose, with focus, with determination, with love, and without being obsessed with oneself," he said. "All that he does is outwardly directed. And he would freely say that the inspiration for all of this is his muse, Jean."

In accepting the award, Jean Trebek drove home Fordham values that align with those of her and her husband.

"We understand how education, and probably more importantly, higher education, is one of the linchpins of society," she said. "The many issues that we currently face are intertwined and affected by the leveling of educational availability."

She said that she and her husband find the very idea of how a scholarship can change a life "awe-inspiring."

"Once we are allowed to have the support that leads to an educated mind, that mind has the opportunity to be open and curious which allows for a fuller understanding and appreciation of our humanity both individually and collectively," she said, noting that she has seen it occur in her own family.

"On a personal note, thank you, Father McShane and Fordham, for helping to develop our son Matthew's personhood, both intellectually and emotionally, so that he can move through his life, which he does, with great confidence, responsibility, and creativity," she said.

Her husband echoed her sentiments.

"If you have compassion in your heart, everything is possible, peace everywhere is possible," he said. "If we are able to affect society in a positive way then our lives will not be for naught."

Father McShane said he could not agree more with the couple, particularly as it related to the power of prayer. He then asked the crowd to join him to pray for Alex and "for his ministry."

"That's the one thing that has become clearer and clearer in the last few months, the school teacher has now become the minister," said Father McShane, before reciting the Our Father and blessing Alex.

Fordham University President Father Joseph McShane blesses Alex Trebek.
(Photograph courtesy of Kait McKay and published with her permission and that of Fordham University.)

THE MAGIC BANK ACCOUNT

By Paul "Bear" Bryant

This was reportedly written by and found in the billfold of Coach Paul "Bear" Bryant of the University of Alabama after he died in 1982. It was emailed to me by my late friend and fellow Marine, George R. "Sully" Sullivan, on December 14, 2019, a few weeks before he passed away. (For more on his life please see "A Message from an Amputee Friend" earlier herein.)

Coach Bryant motivates and inspires us to use our most precious resource wisely.

Imagine that you had won the following *PRIZE* in a contest:

Each morning your bank would deposit $86,400 in your private account for your personal use.
However, this prize has rules. The set of rules are as follow:

1. Everything that you don't spend each day will be taken away from you.
2. You may not simply transfer money into some other account.
3. You may only spend it.
4. Each morning, upon awakening, the bank opens your account with another $86,400 for the new day.
5. The bank can end the game without warning; at any time it can say, "Game Over!" It can close the account and you will not receive a new one.

What would you personally do with your prize?
You would buy anything and everything you wanted right? Not only for yourself, but for all the people you love and care for. Even

for people you don't know, because you couldn't possibly spend it all on yourself, right? You would try to spend every penny, and use it all, because you knew money would be replenished in the morning, right?

Actually, THIS GAME IS REAL. Shocked? Yes! **Each of us is already a winner** of a much more valuable *PRIZE.* We just don't seem to realize it.

The prize is *TIME.*

1. Each morning we awaken to receive 86,400 seconds as a gift of life.
2. And when we go to sleep at night, any remaining time is NOT credited to us.
3. What we haven't used up that day is forever lost.
4. Yesterday is forever gone.
5. Each morning the account is refilled, but the bank can dissolve your account at any time WITHOUT WARNING.

So, ***WHAT WILL YOU DO WITH YOUR 86,400*** seconds today? **Those seconds are worth much, much more than the same amount in dollars**. Think about it and remember to **enjoy every second of your life**, because time races by so much quicker than you think.

So take care of yourself, be happy, love deeply and enjoy life! Here's wishing you a wonderful and beautiful day. Start "spending" your valuable *PRIZE* wisely. The Magic Bank Account is available to us all.

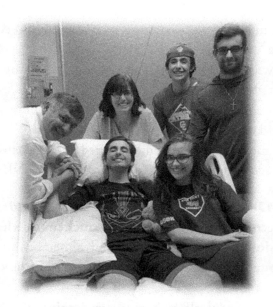

Another great shot of Mansclan with Kevin continuing to recover.
(Photograph courtesy of Dawn Mansfield and published with her permission.)

WHY WOMEN CRY

Author Unknown

Occasionally in life there are those moments of unutterable fulfillment which cannot be completely explained by those symbols called words. Their meanings can only be articulated by the inaudible language of the heart.

— Martin Luther King, Jr.

In the poem below, the words ascribed to "God" are particularly apt in the wake of Kevin's mother Dawn's heroic performance for her son.

A little boy asked his mother,
"Why are you crying?"

"Because I'm a woman," she told him.

"I don't understand," he said.

His Mom just hugged him and said,
"And you never will."

Later the little boy asked his father,
"Why does mother seem to cry for no reason?"

"All women cry for no reason,"
was all his dad could say.

The little boy grew up and became a man,
still wondering why women cry.

Finally he put in a call to God.

MARY ANN AND CHUCK MANSFIELD

When God got on the phone,
he asked,
"God, why do women cry so easily?"

God said:
"When I made the woman she had to be special.
I made her shoulders strong enough to carry the weight of the world,
yet gentle enough to give comfort.
I gave her an inner strength to endure childbirth and the
rejection that many times comes from her children.
I gave her a hardness that allows her to keep
going when everyone else gives up,
and take care of her family through sickness
and fatigue without complaining.
I gave her the sensitivity to love her children
under any and all circumstances,
even when her child has hurt her very badly.
I gave her strength to carry her husband through his faults
and fashioned her from his rib to protect his heart.
I gave her wisdom to know that a good husband never hurts his wife,
but sometimes tests her strengths and her resolve to stand beside him
unfalteringly.
And finally, I gave her a tear to shed. This is hers
exclusively to use whenever it is needed."

"You see my son," said God,
"The beauty of a woman is not in the clothes she wears,
the figure that she carries,
or the way she combs her hair.

The beauty of a woman must be seen in her eyes,
because that is the doorway to her heart - the place where love resides.

THEY NEVER GAVE UP!

By Doyce G. Payne

Courage isn't having the strength to go on – it is going on when you don't have strength.

— Napoleon Bonaparte

Doyce is a retired physician, a true friend and a deeply spiritual person. He and his wife, Kay, are fellow residents of the Sandpebble Beach Condominium on Hutchinson Island, Stuart, Fl. As he has written below, he initiated and led a small group of us in prayer (in the swimming pool!) with the most inspirational and moving words I had heard in years. Indeed, his performance prompted me to tell him, "Doyce, Billy Graham's got nothing on you!" (Reverend Graham had passed away just two days before Kevin was stricken and Doyce prayed for him.)

Thank you, Doyce.

There are many things in life which I feel are universal. A couple being: All life is precious and everyone has an innate will/desire for survival. We learn early that life can throw one doozy of a punch, and finally faith and family are paramount.

On February 23, 2018, the Mansfield family was blindsided. There's an old adage that says, "What doesn't kill you makes you stronger." I know this to be true internally, but not physically (we all have seen the permanent post-stroke sequelae*).

Kay and I were blessed to be with Chuck and other friends in Stuart, Florida, when Mame came and informed us of Kevin's dire situation. Chuck asked for prayer. An overwhelming unspoken voice moved me to say "Let's pray right now." Upon closing the prayer, I again felt God's presence. This time I sensed in my spirit, "Kevin is not going to die." I now regret not sharing that with the others present.

As a Christian, I know that scripture tells us:

1) A day has been set aside for each of us to die.
2) The devil is on a chain.
3) Spiritual blessings come wrapped in trials (James 1:2-4).

I see a Kevin Courageous/Survivor. As noted earlier, we all desire to survive.

God wants us to thrive.

When thinking of Kevin, I'm reminded of the survivors of the infamous Bataan Death march and the late basketball player, coach and broadcaster Jim Valvano. What do they all have in common? **<u>They never gave up!!!</u>** (For inspiration, Google Jim Valvano, 3/3/93 ESPY Courage Award winner.) Kevin didn't give up! He never gave up!

Today we stand amazed at Kevin's courage and desire to survive, all due to his deep love for family, friends and faith.

* According to our online dictionary, sequelae is the plural of sequela, "a pathological condition resulting from a prior disease, injury, or attack."

OUR VILLAGE

By Dawn Chiaramonte Mansfield and Mary Ann Mansfield

"It takes a village to raise a child."

According to www.reference.com, this "is an Igbo and Yoruba proverb that comes from many different African languages. It reflects the emphasis African cultures place on family and community and may have its origins in a biblical worldview."

When Kevin took the awful hit at such an early and formative stage of his life, the outpouring of support from literally thousands of people was overwhelming. Family, friends and strangers offered prayers, financial support, food and encouragement, sharing both time and treasure. Theirs is a story of compassion that includes extraordinary actions to help a young man and his family survive a tragedy. Here, in part, is the background of our "village."

Aside from immediate family members, Mame has four sisters, fourteen nieces and nephews, twenty-one grand-nieces and nephews, and ten in-laws. Chuck has five siblings, one niece, four grand-nieces and nephews, two in-laws and more cousins than he can count! Within five minutes of my notifying only siblings, heaven was under siege. Two of my nephews in the medical field offered calming advice to Chas and Dawn, one took a special trip to visit Kevin in the hospital. Those who could contributed to the GoFundMe page that one of Dawn's colleagues set up; some 200 donors gave. Chuck's first cousin is a Discalced Carmelite who had the Order around the world praying for Kevin's recovery.

Chuck's and Mame's lives have spanned seventy-five years. Those years have seen the "ties that bind," aka love, grow among countless people we are blessed to call friends. Chuck is known as the "Reunion King" mainly because he endeavors to gather friends and their spouses from all stages of his life. Grammar school, high school, college, the Marine Corps, multiple business endeavors, neighbors from the thirteen locations where we lived during our 52+ years of marriage – all were sources from which we drew strength. Most of our friends have followed the Mansfields' adventures through thick and thin, in times of trial and triumph. Their words of comfort gave credence to their unstated motives of "I feel your pain."

Mame was part of a mathematics community derived from teaching at Carle Place High School for 28 years, serving as president of the Nassau County Mathematics Association, and co-chairing the working group of volunteers at the National Museum of Mathematics (MoMath) in New York City. Retired from teaching in 2008, Mame was both shocked and immeasurably grateful for the contributions from former colleagues and students who had shared in the joy when Kevin was born. Perhaps their experience with teenagers and the traumas they helped guide their students through also motivated the concern and generosity for our 18-year old grandson, who was a senior in high school at the time he was taken ill. Two years later, all continue to ask about and pray for Kevin's recovery.

Mame has had a devotion to The Divine Mercy for years and prays its Novena daily. When an ad appeared in the Naples News depicting Christ's image and the words, "Jesus, I trust in You" from "friends of Kevin," we came to believe that "Kevin" referred to our grandson. We have many friends in the Naples area who were aware of his life-threatening illness, and this ad appeared shortly after his diagnosis. Recently, we learned that the same ad is taken out every year by Keith Koenig, owner of City Furniture, to honor his brother Kevin's devotion to The Divine Mercy. No matter, we were convinced that the readers of the ad included our Kevin in their prayers.

Yet, these thousands are largely two generations removed from Kevin and peripheral to the village. Mansclan (as Chas' family is known) is the village center whose members have been part of the story all along. There were forty-two days of alarms beeping, comings and goings, tests/results; through it all, memories of the village's support are vivid, beginning with the extraordinary kindnesses from neighbors, friends and especially the medical personnel.

There was so much food everywhere, meals "our village" delivered every day to home and snacks delivered to the hospital too. Worry that everyone had food to eat was nonexistent because there was always a selection to choose from. One neighbor and friend who made some muffins for us found out that the kids absolutely loved having them (it was an easy grab and go) so she continued to make them. After Kevin came home and she heard he liked them also, she would deliver them to him, straight from the oven.

Justin always bought lunch at school so money was put on his lunch account monthly. When the new month rolled around (the week after Kevin was admitted) he went without lunch. This boy never said anything about it. He just waited until we remembered to replenish his account the following week. One of Justin's friends noticed that he wasn't buying lunch so when his mom made his lunch, he asked her if she would make an extra peanut butter and jelly sandwich for Justin. She did...every day for the remainder of the school year.

The staff in Neuro ICU was amazing. They all loved Kevin and checked on both him and his mother, even if he wasn't their patient that shift. Having spent two weeks there and knowing everyone, Dawn felt comfortable leaving his room for a few minutes at a time, knowing he was always being watched. Since Kevin had played the role of Donkey in his high school musical *Shrek*, his friend brought a stuffed donkey when he first came to see Kevin in ICU. Kevin was still unconscious but somehow held on to this stuffed toy. Donkey stayed by Kevin's side his entire journey. The nurses knew of Donkey and, if they needed to do anything with Kevin, Donkey went along or was placed right back in Kevin's arms as quickly as possible. On a subsequent visit to the ICU staff after Kevin was released from rehab, each nurse received his/her own Donkey from their former patient. It was so special to see how much they loved their gift and even more special to see Kevin up and walking. Too infrequently, these dedicated professionals attended to patients as young as Kevin and witnessed the positive outcome of their treatments. Another reminder just how special these nurses are.

GRATITUDE FOR GOFUNDME AND OTHER DONORS

Here is the introduction to Kevin's GoFundMe web page.

"Kevin Mansfield was a happy kid with an infectious smile and bubbling personality. On Friday, February 23, 2018 all that changed. On this day, his mom came home to take him to the doctor only to find him not responsive. Kevin is currently in Neuro ICU at Presbyterian Medical Center in Charlotte, North Carolina. He has been diagnosed with Acute Necrotizing Encephalopathy Myelitis brought on by the Flu Type B virus. He is only the second documented case of this strain. His immune system is attacking the nerve membranes of his brain forcing him into a coma. With extensive medical treatments, each day brings some excitement as Kevin has started to open his eyes, squeeze hands and wiggle toes on command.

"Kevin's family has embraced the motto, #babysteps and needs our support. All of this has placed a tremendous emotional and financial strain on the family. Even with insurance, the out of pocket expenses are adding up. Except for the standard GOFUNDME and merchant card fees, 100% of the money raised will go towards caring for Kevin with hospital bills and rehabilitation costs. No amount is too small, please consider donating to Kevin and his family as they begin this new journey together.

"Thank you for reading and sharing Kevin's story."

The Mansfield family will ever be grateful to the following persons and the organization for their commitment of financial resources to www.gofundme.com and otherwise for Kevin's benefit.

KEVIN COURAGEOUS

Chloe Allen
Peter Altman
Peyton Alvino
Zach Ambrose
Anonymous Donors
Laura Aquilone
Kevin Arrington
Brian Augustine
Amelia Avellanada and sons (Walter and Christopher)
Karen Barnash
Jane Barnett
Iris Battino
Angela Bauer
Suzanne Bauer
Rebecca Benton
Cyrus Beschloss
Hank Binger
Larry Blackwell
Lara Blair
Gretchen Bottrill
Anne Bowman
Cathy Braund
Sam Brown
Arthur Burns
George Carroll
Angela Chapman
Geoff Chatterton
Diane Chen
Joelle Cohn
David Cote
Jack D
Frances Dattolo
Michael DeAddio
Janine Defeo
Carol Dell'Olio
Christina Del Sesto
Cynthia Dickerson
Joe DiSabato
Hannah Duchardt
Sam Dugdale
Jean Fluett
Tony Fortier-Bensen and Jackie Giammatteo
Kathleen Franek
Regina Gervasi
Jack Gillen
Ellis Glasco
Joel and Jen Glasco
Glenn Godin
Jennifer Leigh Goodman
Nannette Gorman
Maria Grasso
Madeline Greer
Nick Gregor
Cindy Grim
Gail Grim
Paul Grim
Barbara Guidi
Jenny Hackett
Susie Stewart Heinz
Guille Henegar
Daniel Hill
Kate Hindin
John Hipsher
Jennifer Hoefling
Mick Horrocks
Roger and Joanne Hunt
Karen Huth
Betty Ann Huysman
Schuyler Johnson
Allison Kelly
Pete and Mary Kelly
Tom Kiley
Carol and Kevin Kilgallin
Rebecca King
Bill and Mary Kinney
William Kinney
Susan Klat
Sam Koukoulas
Ginny Kunik
David Kwan
Lucy Landesberg
Steve Lanzillotta
Allyson Lavins
Cindy Lawrence
Elizabeth Lazaro
Susan Leatherman
Nancy Lieberman
Nancy Lissemore
Alyssa/Christopher Lokey
Dan Lomas
Conor Lourey
Christian Lucas
Doug Lucas
Bob and Patty Lund
Joseph and Margaret Luongo
Danielle Magno
Peggy Mansfield
Tim Mansfield
Joan Marrinan
Lorraine and Mike Matthews
Kiko Mawougbe
Marie McCann
Shaun McConoughey
Renee McDonald
Maryann McKeon
Danielle Meehan
Frank Mele
The Merchels
Craig and Terry Middleton
Eleanore Miechkowski
Mikulus Family
Judith Mize
Kieran C. Morris
Anke Muench
JoJo Muir
Nicholas Muniz

Cathy Murphy
Emilia Murphy
Ali Naderi
NCMTA
Kristin Neal
Mike Nicoll
Jim Norwood
Shirley and Mark Orton
Sue Osward
Claire Pendleton
Emma Pixley
Pixley Family
Lukman Ramsey
Candace Roane
Jack Roberts
Jim Robinson
Lee Rockford
Therese Roland
Steve Root
Susan and Ed Rubin

Landon Rudd
Mary Rutkowski
Laura, Ken and Kimberly
Ryan
Betsy Scarisbrick
Doug Schaffer
David Schroder
Bill and Berta Schroeder
David Schroeder
Maggie Schroeder
Michele Seaman
Mallory Seibel
Jack Shannon
Byron Shaw
Gina Sheppard
Elise Siegel
Cathy Siliakus
Kim Louise Smith
Alexis Stevens
Brady Stevens

Pat Stevens
Laura Stevenson
Trevor Stricker
Morgan Swift
Mary Taylor
Ann Carmen Thomas
Alfred Tom
Michelle Tosas
Bob and Keli Trejo
Jane Tronco
Debbie and Bob Tyler
Linda Walsh
Sherry Wang
Tara Byron Williams
Bryan Woolley
Cynthia Zente
Barbara Ziminski
Howard and Carol Zolla

A MOTHER'S MUSINGS

By Dawn Chiaramonte Mansfield

Two years later, some memories of the traumatic period from February 23 until April 5, 2018, are still vivid and recounted here by Kevin's mother.

Food, Food, and Did I Mention Food!

The hospital French fries became our main sustenance. We talked about how much Kevin would love them when he could finally have solid food again. (French fries were a staple of Kevin's diet before 2/23.) He couldn't wait. Unfortunately for us, someone in hospital management had the bright idea that fried foods were not healthy and, therefore, foods, formerly fried, would henceforth be baked. Baked, healthy?! We were in the midst of a trauma and needed comfort food. Who wanted baked fries? Besides, they were horrible. When we talk about those fries, Kevin still resents that he never got the chance to try them.

Kevin was/is famous among friends and family for his picky eating habits. If he likes a food he can and will eat a lot of it, but those choices are slim. Steak and chicken breast (maybe with a little barbecue sauce), rotini pasta, and only certain chicken nuggets or pizza make his dietary list. He loves carbs! His eating habits gave inspiration for this ditty: *If it's green, he'll scream. If it's a fruit, give it the boot!*

When he was finally allowed to start eating food, most was pureed or ground due to his swallowing issues. Pieces got bigger as he mastered the skill of swallowing without choking or aspirating. Unbelievably, this child was eating foods like meatloaf and carrots and bananas. (Still no green foods, except maybe a few peas.) The family was thrilled to be going home with more food options. The hope was dashed over time, however. He would, and still does, insist that he never ate them or liked them, except the bananas, and won't even try them again to remind himself.

With all the food coming and going and the family all doing their best to make sure it got stored properly, one small bag of snacks with a selection of chips and cookies was put in the garage. Somehow, the bag went unnoticed and over time was just pushed aside. Several months later, as the garage was being cleared, the bag was found. Mansclan may not have enjoyed its contents, but they are confident in saying that the little mouse, who ate himself to death, did. He had eaten every chip and cookie in that big brown bag! May he rest in peace!

<u>Doctors and Nurses and Staff, Oh My</u>

Cleveland, Ohio, proved to be the source of Kevin's diagnosis. The doctors in Charlotte were still trying to figure out what was going on in Kevin's body when his neurologist contacted her mentor in Cleveland to ask his opinion. He previously had had a case exactly like Kevin's. Kevin is only the second documented case of Acute Necrotizing Encephalopathy Myelitis from Strain B of the flu. What is that you ask? In layman's terms, the post infection from the flu was causing his immune system to attack the myelin (covering of the nerves) in his brain. If you research the disease, not much has been written about it. (*Authors' note: Please see ANEM Not AMEN earlier in this work.*)

Once the doctor was sure of Kevin's diagnosis, she convened the family to discuss what was happening. She reminded us that when Kevin wakes up, we may not have the same Kevin. Thoughts ranged from, 'Hmm, you mean maybe he won't be so picky when eating? Okay! Maybe he won't be so stubborn? Okay! A change in Kevin may not be that bad.' If that sounds harsh, trying to be light-hearted was a reaction to a stressful or nervous situation. Kevin did change some. Growing up, he wasn't a huggy-feely kind of guy. He was sensitive and wore his heart on his sleeve, but it took a lot to get close. Now, he is much more affectionate and loving towards his family, kisses his mother goodnight and hugs with feeling. What a wonderful change!

Dawn hated leaving ICU to go to the Step-Down Unit where she didn't know anyone and came to find out that most of that staff were traveling nurses. Never seeing the same nurse twice, the family was informed that nurses checked on patients every two to three hours unless they pressed the call button. Every two to three hours for a person who can barely talk, can't walk or do anything for himself, including press the call button?! It was at that point that the decision was made: Kevin would never be left alone again for the rest of his time there. Not even for a minute!

The first night in his new room, Kevin got a severe nosebleed. With a feeding tube in his nose, it was not easy to stop. Pressing the call button, and expressing the urgent need for a nurse, given what was happening, the two waited…and waited…and waited. With Kevin now covered in blood and his mother fuming, a nurse walked in with no urgency at all. She nonchalantly said she needed some towels, left abruptly and seemed to take an inordinate amount of time before reappearing. After she cleaned Kevin, Dawn recalls, "I sat looking at him wondering what would have happened if I weren't there. I had made the mistake once of not being there for him. It wouldn't happen again. I did bring it to the nurse's attention that he was unable to do anything for himself and if we needed her it was for a good reason. Fast forward a couple of hours and the same thing happened. You would have hoped that when we called the second time, she would have put a little pep in her step. I was so upset thinking of other patients who might have been in a similar situation who didn't have anybody there with them."

Parting is Such Sweet Sorrow…

The anxiously awaited day arrived for Tim to leave for France. He had worked his whole life towards that goal: Beginning a professional baseball career. But when Tim went to say goodbye to Kevin, his resolve could have changed in one quick moment. Kevin had never been so emotional, crying uncontrollably and hanging onto his brother for dear life. The heartbreaking response was almost cause for Tim to cancel his trip. Only a promise to let him know if there were any changes or reason for him to come home convinced him to go. Tim was emotional leaving and Kevin was inconsolable for the entire day. As I sat with my distraught son on his bed, I admit thinking, "How much more could this boy take?"

TWO YEARS AFTER THE WORST DAY

By Dawn Chiaramonte Mansfield

You must be the change you want to see in the world.

– Mahatma Ghandi

Dawn wrote this reflection on February 23, 2020, two years to the day after Kevin was stricken with flu-induced Acute Necrotizing Encephalopathy Myelitis (ANEM). Her tone is on of gratitude, realism, acceptance and good cheer.

Two years after the worst day of our lives. Two years after not knowing if my son would live or die. Two years later and I am ever so grateful now.

Grateful for our village. Those that still check in on Kevin. Those that help bring him to appointments, keep him company and those who still keep him in their prayers.

Grateful for my children who treat Kevin like nothing has happened, yet know his limitations, and don't make him feel different.

Grateful for my rock, my husband, my best friend. The man who travels for work every week but when home makes sure he takes the load off me so I have some time off.

Most grateful for Kevin, who never gave up.

Kevin two years later.
(Photograph courtesy of Dawn Mansfield and published with her permission.)

Kevin went through a psychological evaluation this past year and it was stated that he is permanently and completely disabled. He continues with occupational and cognitive therapy, usually three times a week. He still has tremors in both hands, although the right has improved some while the left not much at all. He recently had five injections of Botox in his left arm to try and help lessen the tremors. The neurologist has said that his type of tremors is the hardest to control. So far, the Botox does not seem to be doing anything.

His short term memory is hit or miss. He has learned to use alarms to remind him to do certain things. He and "Alexa" have become very good friends. His therapists and doctors are all amazing and know what he can't do and when to push him.

Tim moved home last week and started working out with Kevin to get him stronger and add some muscle on that body. He has only regained about half of the 30 pounds he lost.

We recently moved into our new house and Kevin has settled in nicely. We now need to reapply for Vocational Rehabilitation in Union County. Once that is complete, we can start looking into Kevin taking some online classes.

KEVIN COURAGEOUS

Not sure what the future holds for Kevin, but two years after the worst day of our lives, it sure looks a whole lot brighter!

❤*baby steps can be taken at any age.*

"INVICTUS"

By William Ernest Henley

According to Wikipedia, Mr. Henley (1849–1903) "was an influential poet, critic and editor of the late-Victorian era in England who is spoken of as having as central a role in his time as Samuel Johnson had in the eighteenth century. He is remembered most often for his 1875 poem 'Invictus,' a piece which recurs in popular awareness (e.g., see the 2009 Clint Eastwood film, Invictus). It is one of his hospital poems from early battles with tuberculosis and is said to have developed the artistic motif of poet as a patient, and to have anticipated modern poetry in form and subject matter."

For me the last two lines of Mr. Henley's powerful poem constitute an apt summary of my life, and I hope it resonates with Kevin, his family and all who read this.

Here is "Invictus," which is Latin for 'unconquered.'

Out of the night that covers me,
Black as the pit from pole to pole,
I thank whatever gods may be
For my unconquerable soul.
In the fell clutch of circumstance
I have not winced nor cried aloud.
Under the bludgeonings of chance
My head is bloody, but unbowed.
Beyond this place of wrath and tears
Looms but the Horror of the shade,
And yet the menace of the years
Finds and shall find me unafraid.
It matters not how strait the gate,

How charged with punishments the scroll,
I am the master of my fate,
I am the captain of my soul.

Invictus!
*(Photograph courtesy of Dawn Mansfield and
published with her permission.)*

HERE AND NOW: IN HIS OWN WORDS

By Kevin Sean Mansfield Assisted by His Dad

Life may not be the party we hoped for... but while we're here we may as well dance.

— Jeanne C. Stein

    Kevin's father, Chas, conducted this interview approximately two years after Kevin fell ill. In Kevin's words you will find frustration, fear, disappointment, gratitude, realism, faith, hope and love. And this courageous young man does not feel sorry for himself.

Q: When you think about your ordeal, what thoughts do you have?
Kevin: At times, it's really annoying.

Q: What is?
Kevin: I used to be able to do things, but now I can't. Like writing, for example. In my mind, I used to be able to write and, suddenly, I can't. At least not well.

Q: Does it make you mad?
Kevin: Not really. More like frustrated.

Q: What or when is the first time you remember that frustration?
Kevin: Probably when I was in the in-patient rehab. I was trying to dribble a ball. It should have been easy; I used to do it all the time! I remember the therapists asking me to do things I knew I could do before I got sick but I couldn't anymore.

Q: Anything else?
Kevin: I remember getting frustrated at how tired it would make me just to walk around.

Q: What do you remember immediately before getting sick?
Kevin: I remember spraining my ankle but I don't have any sense of timing or when it happened. I remember wearing a walking boot and I remember kissing [a friend].

Q: Do you recall your reaction as people first tried to explain to you what had happened?
Kevin: Yes. I did not believe them. It seemed impossible and did not make sense.

Q: Do you know what exactly happened?
Kevin: My brain swelled. My thalamus was damaged.

Q: Do you know what the thalamus impacts?
Kevin: I think my stamina throughout the day is reduced and my fine motor skills are not good.

Q: What do you remember from the hospital/rehabilitation center?
Kevin: Nothing from the ICU at all. I remember quite a bit from the rehab. My memories from the step-down unit are spotty and vague. I remember Mamie coming to visit me and I remember my siblings complaining about the lack of parking.

Q: When you were told that your disability was "permanent" and "complete," what was your reaction?
Kevin: I wasn't shocked at the permanence. I have kind of come to accept that my life is going to be different. But to hear the doctor that evaluated me for Social Security benefits tell me my disability was complete, that I would never be able to earn a living, really made me angry. I felt like, "#&@% you! What gives you the ability to dictate I am #&@%ed for life?!" I know I can't write. I know I have substantial physical impairments but I don't feel like I am unable to EVER earn a living.

Q: What about speech-to-text? Does that help with writing or notes?
Kevin: Not really. Siri usually misunderstands me. The technology just isn't reliable enough yet.

Q: What frustrates you these days?
Kevin: Writing. I just don't understand why it is so difficult. I learned it once. I know how to do it but my hand just doesn't respond.

Q: Do you feel sorry for yourself?
Kevin: Not really. It is more confusion. I really don't understand why it happened to me. I don't feel sorry for myself but it still doesn't make sense to me.

Q: So you realize there is nothing you did to "deserve this," right?
Kevin: Of course! It does reflect my luck though. Things just seem to go wrong for me more often than for others.

Q: How about memories before your illness?
Kevin: Oh, yeah. I remember being on stage, singing and dancing. I remember being with friends. I remember kissing people. I remember being a normal teenager. I really loved performing.

Q: Would you ever perform again?
Kevin: I doubt it. I know I can't move like I used to. I don't feel like I respond on time. I doubt I will be able to memorize lines. I used to love performing but it came naturally. I doubt I could still do it well because of my physical disabilities.

Q: What vision do you have for your future?
Kevin: Right now, I don't know.

Q: What about relationships or marriage?
Kevin: Maybe. I would like to have a girlfriend and maybe get married. It's hard to see that right now but I am hopeful.

Q: What about children?
Kevin: No. I don't see how I could be a good father with my current disabilities. I would not want to put that on my wife. Maybe that will change but I don't see how I could do the job right now.

Q: Is there anything about your new life that you like?
Kevin: I like living at home without paying rent. I like the fact that I live with people. I'm really frightened by living alone because of what happened. I hate to think if I had been home alone. I am really thankful to be alive. This event brought my siblings and me closer. I am really thankful for my Mom and Dad.

Q: At this point, what do you think will improve?
Kevin: I hope my speech improves. I feel like it keeps getting better. I also hope the timing of my jokes improves [laughs].

Q: What would your perfect life look like?
Kevin: I would live in Golden Oak (a luxury residential community on the grounds of Walt Disney World). I would be a billionaire investor and the GM of the New York Giants. The guy who's got that job now is a total bum!

Q: As you follow or look at your old friends, what are your thoughts?
Kevin: Damn, they're getting old! I know I have gotten older too but they are going to college, starting careers while I am not. I'm not upset, but I think about them from high school.

Q: What about college for you?
Kevin: Not now. I'm afraid of college right now, especially after the shooting at UNCC last year. I have plenty I need to learn and maybe I will need to go in like ten years. If I need to go to college so I can support myself, I will.

Q: What relationships from your old life have continued to expand in your new life?
Kevin: Other than my siblings, only Annie (Grim). She introduced me to her boyfriend and I really like him. I think he is a good guy who respects her. All her other boyfriends were disdainful.

Q: How about your relationship with your parents?
Kevin: My relationship with Mom is really good. That is usually better than before I got sick. Conversations with Dad are more intense.

Q: Do you remember when Tim left for France to play baseball?
Kevin: Oh yeah! I was so sad. I really was afraid for him to go. I felt like I was never going to see him again. I just cried and cried. I am so glad he is living at home now.

Q: Do you realize how many people care about you?
Kevin: I didn't used to. Now I do. I realize how many people were praying for me. I am amazed at how many people donated money for me. I'm really grateful. People still tell me how much they care about me and pray for me. In fact, I have come to expect people to consider me the center of attention, and I am shocked when the focus is on someone else.

Q: What is the scariest thing you remember or have seen from your hospital stay?
Kevin: I really get upset when I see the picture of me in a coma with tubes and wires everywhere. The whole thing is really disgusting. I also get really upset when I hear about people's reactions to my coma. I start crying when you, Mom or Mamie and Poppa talk about your fears and panic.

Q: What is the funniest memory or story from your hospital stay?
Kevin: The fart gun that Shirley (Orton) brought me. That would make me laugh constantly. I also never get tired of the story when I told you, "Don't fart with your pants down."

Q: Have you been trying your hardest to recover?
Kevin: In my therapy sessions, yes. Honestly, outside of therapy I don't make maximum effort. I ask people to help me with things I could probably do myself. Also, when I do my therapy homework, I will do my exercises once, but I don't do the level of repetition that doctors and therapists want me to.

Q: Why don't you try your best?
Kevin: Fear of falling short. If I don't get better, I have the excuse that I did not try my best. If I try my best and don't get better, then I will be really frustrated and disappointed.

Q: Do you feel the movement that is impaired?
Kevin: I am really aware that I am moving slower than I used to. But I'm not trying to move slower. In my mind I am moving at the same speed I always have; my body just doesn't react the way it always has. Know that I am moving as fast as I can.

Q: Do you believe in God?
Kevin: Yes. I believe there is a reason why this happened; we just don't know what it is yet. We may never know; maybe we will though… I have learned to live one day at a time. Don't waste too much energy on the distant future because you might be unconscious with a swollen brain. Some people care, some don't. When things like this happen, the true friends are revealed. People I thought were friends really were not. There was a whole community of people from Charlotte Catholic theater that I thought would be lifelong friends. They weren't. I don't blame them but I am surprised.

EPILOGUE

'A lot has changed in this year. Kevin has made some great strides. His strength is amazing. … Today, one year later, I am eternally grateful…for Kevin being here with us…for my family who has gotten through this stronger…for our village whom we will never be able to thank enough…and most importantly, I am so grateful that God has given me the chance to spend more time with my son." So wrote Kevin's mother Dawn in the foreword to this work in February of 2019.

We might simply write "Amen" at this point. Still, we believe there are risks to be faced in every moment of our lives, and risk avoidance or evasion has never been anyone's right or privilege. Accordingly, as stated in the preface hereto, "And so, we share the 'Kevin' stories of family, friends and strangers. They are filled with faith in the power of prayer, hope for a happy ending, and love for a courageous young man who will overcome the tragedies on his life's journey." May it quickly come to pass.

One applicable lesson for all of us can be found in words written long ago by a now deceased friend, Paul Gillcrist: "If talented people are challenged with tough but achievable goals, and if they are given the leeway to act on their own, with adequate support, they can, and will, work wonders."

Kevin, the wonders lie ahead.

Kevin with Mamie and Poppa in Charlotte, N.C., Christmas 2018.
(Photograph courtesy of Dawn Mansfield and published with her permission.)

ABOUT THE AUTHORS

In a career spanning more than thirty years, Mary Ann Mansfield contributed to mathematics education both in the classroom as an innovator and outside it as a motivator and instructor of colleagues. She consistently updated her teaching techniques to accommodate changes in mathematics education and was recognized for her outstanding efforts by students, colleagues and professionals, even in peripheral fields. Currently co-chair of the Working Group of the Museum of Mathematics (MOMATH), Mary Ann has assisted in the writing of an educators' guide for the Museum's traveling exhibit, *Math Midway*. She is also a member of the advisory committee for the Math Midway 2 Go (MM2GO) project, an ongoing effort to bring hands-on activities into the classroom to stimulate math learning and enjoyment. Her hobbies include cooking, reading, water aerobics and traveling.

Chuck Mansfield graduated with honors from Chaminade High School (Mineola, N.Y.) in 1962. Upon graduation in 1966 from the College of the Holy Cross with an A.B. (Sociology), he was commissioned an officer in the U.S. Marine Corps Reserve. In 1968 he was assigned to Vietnam and served as a platoon commander with the Third Marine Division. Later, he received an M.B.A. (Finance) from New York University, and served in finance in the U.S. and abroad. A director/trustee of the mutual funds of Federated Hermes, Inc., a $584-billion Pittsburgh-based complex listed on the New York Stock Exchange, he has served in that capacity since 1999 and chaired the board's audit committee for four years.

The couple has been married for 53 years and lives in Stuart, Fl., and Westhampton Beach, N.Y.

CPSIA information can be obtained
at www.ICGtesting.com
Printed in the USA
BVHW031748130520
579652BV00002B/4/J